THE RESPONSIBILITY OF THE PHILOSOPHER

GIANNI VATTIMO

THE RESPONSIBILITY
OF THE PHILOSOPHER

Edited with an Introduction by **FRANCA D'AGOSTINI**
Translated by **WILLIAM MCCUAIG**

COLUMBIA UNIVERSITY PRESS NEW YORK

COLUMBIA UNIVERSITY PRESS

Publishers Since 1893

New York   Chichester, West Sussex

Originally published in Italian as *Vocazione e responsabilità del filosofo*

Copyright © 2000 Gianni Vattimo

Translation copyright © 2010 Columbia University Press

Library of Congress Cataloging-in-Publication Data

Vattimo, Gianni, 1936–

[Vocazione e responsabilita del filosofo. English]

The responsibility of the philosopher / Gianni Vattimo ; edited with an introduction by Franca D'Agostini ; translated by William McCuaig.

p. cm.

Includes bibliographical references and index.

ISBN 978-0-231-15242-6 (cloth : alk. paper)—ISBN 978-0-231-52712-5 (ebook)

1. Philosophy, Modern—20th century.   2. Philosophy, Italian—20th century.   I. D'Agostini, Franca, 1952–   II. Title.

B3654.V383V6313 2010

190—dc22   2010003075

♾

Columbia University Press books are printed on permanent and durable acid-free paper.

This book is printed on paper with recycled content.
Printed in the United States of America

c   10 9 8 7 6 5 4 3 2 1

References to Internet Web sites (URLs) were accurate at the time of writing. Neither the author nor Columbia University Press is responsible for URLs that may have expired or changed since the manuscript was prepared.

CONTENTS

THE RESPONSIBILITY OF THE PHILOSOPHER

INTRODUCTION: THE STRONG REASONS FOR WEAK THOUGHT

Franca D'Agostini

There exist thinkers—Kierkegaard and Hannah Arendt come especially to mind—whose propensity for singularity and antitheory is grounded in precise and rigorously theoretical reasons. This to a certain extent is Gianni Vattimo's case too, and the primary aim of what follows is to bring out the strong reasons for Vattimo's commitment to "weak thought" (*pensiero debole*), and to an "attenuation" or "lightening" of the structures of traditional philosophical discourse.[1]

Attenuation and lightening are not self-explanatory notions when applied to philosophy. To lighten or pare down a theory generally means strengthening the logical power of the theory itself (a point made promptly by acute critics of Vattimo like Carlo A. Viano and Enrico Berti). Actually, when the formula was coined, it conveyed a meaning more associative than argumentative. The expression "weak thought" was quite clearly a catchphrase meant to characterize, and render historically intelligible, the aftermath of an unpleasantly shallow and cruel climate that had come about in philosophy and political thought in the second half of the 1970s.

At that time, the analyses of such neostructuralist thinkers as Deleuze and Foucault were picked up in Italy and fused into an "explosive mixture," in which a fundamental aestheticism, cut-rate and insouciant, was coupled with a certain facility in taking up arms, or rhetoricizing about the "armed struggle." What was going on, and what did it mean, philosophically speaking? Vattimo's answer was both radical and reasonable: following Nietzsche and Heidegger, he applied the term "nihilism" to this historical mix of aestheticism and terrorism, and weak thought was put forward as philosophy's response in the face of this state of affairs. Weak thought is thus, very simply, the right way to do philosophy in the epoch (and amid the contingencies) of nihilism. Weak thought and nihilism are two basic notions with which some familiarity is needed in order to grasp Vattimo's philosophical position. They sound oddly strident if taken together, and yet, right there lies the key, I believe, to the meaning of just what it is that Vattimo is proposing with this thought-combination. The nihilist temperament is an icy passion, passionless out of inner passion, while weak thought seems like the soft but calculated negation of any passion at all—or any iciness either. The two attitudes may be reciprocally corrective, or either may be promoted at the expense of the other. So while Vattimo's theoretical stance may be vulnerable to a charge of elasticity,[2] its roots are anything but arbitrary and irresponsible, and it comes into sharp focus if we return to the meaning of "lightening" and ask ourselves: what would it signify to weaken, not this or that theory (so incurring the well-founded objections of Viano and Berti), but to weaken that vaste and vague metatheoretical horizon to which our tradition gives the name "philosophy"? To put it another way: what would it mean to posit that there is a specific weakness of philosophy in the epoch of realized nihilism, and that this debility ought to be embraced on compelling (if not "strong") metaphilosophical grounds?

By "weak" Vattimo seems to mean essentially two things: pluralistic and incomplete.[3] Each term corresponds to a critical axis of theoretical discourse; each is a possible path to the dissolution of theory. The first evokes synchronicity (many theses, many "truths," many interpretations are simultaneously legitimate) the second diachronicity (no text, no truth can be said to be definitive and conclusive), hence they correspond to two classic forms of relativism: epistemological and historical.

But there is more to it than that. Weak thought isn't some sort of amalgamated, all-purpose relativism; it's a calculated combination of different modes of relativism in order to get to somewhere else beyond relativism. The meaning of this "beyond" is what Vattimo, through Nietzsche and Heidegger, is seeking. And the (transtheoretical) theory that results should be read primarily, and precisely, as a specific interpretation of "beyond," of what it is in philosophy to surpass and be surpassed, of the way in which, in philosophy, every rigorous surpassing never achieves a higher level, but falls back into the surpassed.[4] Or rather: in philosophy, as soon as you attain a second level, any further attempt to surpass that level tends to fall back into the first, such that philosophical arithmetic would comprise no more than three terms, of which the third is just a new first.[5] This is a basic dialectic, which can be seen as the leitmotiv of all Vattimo's work, and more generally of hermeneutics.[6]

Actually, what makes philosophical discourse specifically weak in Vattimo's sense is not properly the double constatation of the plurality and incompleteness of truth, but rather the constatation of the incompleteness and plurality of this constatation as well. Weak thought in this sense is a third-level description, well synthesized in aphorism 22 from *Beyond Good and Evil* (to which Vattimo himself refers below), in which Nietzsche maintains that all is interpretation (because "each thing follows its own rule"), and if someone objects that this too is an interpretation, the answer will not be to argue back, but to say: so what?

From the perspective of weak thought, we then have three theses arrayed in reflexive steps:

V_0 = "everything is interpretation"

followed immediately by:

V_1 = "V_0 is also an interpretation"

and finally by the admission, the typical starting point of weak thought, that:

V_2 = "we must inevitably think this self-refuting game"

The unaccomplished nihilist, according to Nietzsche, is he or she who stops at the first thesis; the accomplished nihilist is he or she who dares admit the second as well. The typical intonation of hermeneutic nihilism corresponds to the third position, which evidently moves the plane of the discourse beyond the simple description of facts (V_0 does in effect tell us something about the structure of reality, even if what it tells us is rather discouraging for any project to describe reality) but also beyond the description of descriptions. (The critico-transcendental level, indicated here by V_1, does ultimately tell us something about the way we describe reality, even if what it tells us is particularly discouraging for any project aimed at transcendental description.)

V_2 is actually a description of facts, like V_0 (in this respect we can be said to have "fallen back" to the first level), but the facts in question are no longer the simple facts of knowledge and experience, but rather *historico-linguistic events*: what the hermeneutics of Gadamer and Dilthey identifies in the Hegelian "objective spirit." V_2 says to us: nihilism, that is to say the play of overtaking (all is interpretation, this too is an interpretation, so what?) is folded as an intrinsic necessity into every rigorous and "accomplished" attempt to speak the modes of our experience of reality, of the world, and of Being.

Readers will have spotted the reversal, or better the *transvaluation*, performed with V_2: "we must inevitably" signifies "we cannot not—," or "we are compelled to recognize that—." Hence it signifies that there is a theoretical, philosophical necessity to be reckoned with, even if the necessity in question is of a quite particular kind (not for nothing does it arise "coherently" from the *ubiquity* of interpretation, in other words from thesis V_0). This, I believe, is where Vattimo's antifoundationalism diverges from other forms of postmodern and deconstructionist antifoundationalism.[7] At just this point, and unexpectedly, weak thought rejoins the Kierkegaardism of Luigi Pareyson, which was the opposite of "weak" (in the everyday sense of the term).[8] Here lies the strong ground of weak thought, and the generative core of Vattimo's philosophical work.

Vattimo is one of the philosophers best placed to address the question of the role of philosophy at the start of the third millennium,[9] not just because the self-understanding of philosophy has always been one of his favorite themes, but also because his thinking about the topic has been singularly generative and positive.

The passage schematized above with V_0, V_1, V_2 is virtually self-refuting; to regard it as the point of departure of a certain (if not a "new") philosophical practice in the contemporary (technological) world is both a courageous move and a piece of dialectical subtlety of a specific kind. It is not surprising that Vattimo should feel particularly drawn to Christianity from a philosophical point of view: in a way, the strictures to love one's enemy, and to let the weeds[10]grow, find a good, albeit highly decontextualized, application here.[11]

Because "weak" is such an equivocal term, and for other contingent reasons, Vattimo's philosophical project has often run the risk of being misunderstood precisely where its best qualities lie. In fact, if the outcome of his work were only a generic attenuation of theoretical discourse, then a lot of effort was expended for a meager result. But since 1983, the date when the famous collection of essays bearing the title *Il pensiero debole* was published, Vattimo has focused exclusively on elaborating his position and marking it off from a generic attenuation of theory.

The first chapter of *Beyond Interpretation*, entitled "The Nihilistic Vocation of Hermeneutics," is in this respect quite an important text, because it shows clearly how far from "weak" the horizon that justifies the option for weak thought is. Vattimo endeavors to show the irreducibility of hermeneutics to a vague philosophy of culture, and manages this not by emphasizing the Kantism of the philosophical roots of hermeneutics (normally, bringing neo-Kantians back to Kant means bringing philosophies of life, history, and culture back to their good old transcendental—that is, properly and rigorously "philosophical"—roots), but by demonstrating that these philosophical roots cannot be traced back to a Kantian or neo-Kantian sense of objectivity. Vattimo writes:

> What reduces hermeneutics to a generic philosophy of culture is the wholly metaphysical claim (often implicit and unrecognized) to be a finally true description of the (permanent) "interpretative structure" of human existence. The contradictory character of this claim must be taken seriously and a rigorous reflection on the historicity of hermeneutics, in both senses of the genitive, developed on the basis of it. Hermeneutics is not only a theory of the historicity (horizons) of truth: it is itself a radically historical truth.[12]

In other words: from the constatation of the interpretative structure of human existence, taken not as a descriptive constatation, but as itself an interpretation, there emerge the conditions of a "rigorous reflection." "Accomplished" nihilism does not stop at the nihilistic nature of theory, but pushes further and accepts the nihilistic nature of metatheory. The upshot is not in the least a dissolution of theoretical discourse, but on the contrary, and explicitly, the paradoxical "rigor" of weak thought. The necessity of doing away with any metaphysical description leads to contradiction (as this same necessity ought to require a descriptive ground). But it is the awareness of this fact that locates philosophy on the narrow, "risk-laden" crest of interpretation. This, you might say, is the *force majeure* that dictates the thesis of weakening.

The concept of nihilism has been methodologically prominent from the outset of Vattimo's philosophical trajectory and confrontation with Nietzsche, a confrontation that brought him, while still a young man, to the conference at Royaumont in 1964, at which the postwar Nietzsche Renaissance was, so to speak, institutionalized.[13] The current of thought later labelled neostructuralism or poststructuralism emerged clearly at that meeting for perhaps the first time, and went on to become dominant in Europe and subsequently in North America, exerting considerable influence on the theoretical and political evolution of Marxism in that period. It also had a profound influence on what, by the end of the 1970s, began to be seen as a divergence or contrast of philosophical styles: the so-called continental style, as opposed to the analytical one.[14] It was Vattimo's deep awareness of the meaning of nihilism (in Nietzsche and Heidegger) that set him apart ever more clearly from poststructuralist theory, immunizing him in particular against the risk of aestheticism. This risk thinkers of unquestionable importance like Deleuze and Derrida chose to incur, and while it imparts a quite distinctive *esprit* to their writings, it also leaves them marked by a *coquetterie* of a somewhat outdated and geographically restricted kind.[15]

Like Deleuze, Vattimo aimed from the start at an affirmative interpretation of the Nietzschean discourse on nihilism.

So Vattimo and Deleuze can both claim to be "affirmative nihilists" (with the full weight of contradiction that this obviously entails). But there is an important difference. Deleuze (since *Nietzsche and Philosophy*, 1962[16]) pursued a critique of culture that ultimately turned into culture itself, that is to say into the encyclopedic reconstruction he went on to undertake with *Mille Plateaux*. Vattimo appears to take the affirmative interpretation of Nietzsche proposed by Deleuze (and Lyotard) in a nonvitalistic and nonnaturalistic sense. Affirmativity for him is *saying yes to the logoi*, to language and its capacity to express Being, rather than saying yes to "life"—a notion that in this setting seems to be at least as abstract as that from which it wants to distinguish itself. This stance, fundamentally Hegelian and Gadamerian, saves Vattimo from the sort of suicidal contradiction typical of anti-intellectual positions, and detectable in certain pages of Nietzsche himself. (What's the ultimate purpose, one asks oneself, of employing so much force of intellect and language and logos to destroy the logos and demean the intellect?[17])

Thus the interpretation and use that Vattimo makes of nihilism (and of Nietzsche in general) assume their own distinct profile vis-à-vis the French thinkers, and in contrast to the French thinkers, as he searches for some deeper theoretico-philosophical "coherence."[18]

NIHILISM AND DIFFERENCE

A first essential step is taken by the essays collected in *The Adventure of Difference* in 1980.[19] Here, especially in

"Nietzsche and Difference," Vattimo illustrates a certain development of the notion of difference in Heidegger: from a plane we may call "metaphysical" to a plane that we could call *logical* or *methodological*.[20] Vattimo notes that in *Sein und Zeit* (1927; *Being and Time*), and in the subsequent essay "Vom Wesen des Grundes" (1929; "On the Essence of Ground"),[21] Heidegger defines difference essentially as the widening bifurcation between "ontic" and "ontological." In other words: difference is primarily the divergence of Being from beings (existent, present things), such that the truth of things (*a-letheia*) lies in its "not-being-concealed." From this elementary, structural datum, there evidently follows the distinction between two *modes* in which truth eventuates, the ontic (concerning the being of single individuated things "at the disposal" of humans for use and manipulation) and the ontological (concerning Being as such). Hence—as in the Heideggerian *démarche* overall—an essential linkage arises between ontology and methodology, which leads to a radical redefinition of both: ontic designates an analysis focused on the way of being of some present thing or other in front of me (*Vorhandenheit*), while "ontological" is the understanding of "Being qua Being." Vattimo interprets the relation of Heidegger to the French school in light of this connection between ontology and method, showing how French philosophy of difference errs in its interpretation and use of Heidegger (and Nietzsche). He writes:

> *The difference Heidegger is talking about here is the one that always obtains between that which appears within*

a certain horizon, and the horizon itself as an open aper-
ture [apertura aperta] *that makes possible the very ap-*
pearance of existent things.[22]

Hence we are apparently dealing with a metaphysical perspective, that is to say a description of reality "as such," "in
itself." But it should be noted that the descriptivity involved
here is of a transcendental type (corresponding, that is, to
level V_{l}). Here difference is not established between the existent thing and another "thing" to which we could apply the
term "Being," but rather between existent things and Being
as their *transcendental*, as the "open aperture that makes
possible the very appearance of existent things." Vattimo is
thus careful to take Heidegger's neo-Kantianism into account, whereas this seems to have eluded the French thinkers, with consequences we shall see.

In Heidegger the notion of difference does not develop in
this direction; rather, difference itself is foregrounded
and problematized as such. This can be seen in the con-
cluding section of Being and Time, *where the issue is*
raised as a question about why difference has been
forgotten.... Here the problem of ontological difference
is not conceived in reference to what it distinguishes
and the reasons and modalities of distinction. Rather,
it may be translated into the question: "what about
difference?" ... The problem of difference is the problem
that concerns difference itself, not the problem of what
its terms and causes are.[23]

Here Vattimo palpably decouples Heidegger's discourse from any onticizing misunderstanding. In so doing he steers the question toward a dimension no longer properly ontological, but rather logical, or even "functional." What counts in difference is the differing itself, not the instances that may eventuate on either side of the differing. But note: French thinkers, Deleuze as much as Derrida and each in his own way,[24] also promoted a similar shift, discussing the ontological rigidification of differing in Heidegger. Deleuze especially questioned Heidegger's "Oedipal" affection for the *sole* difference, the one between Being and existent beings, where closer attention to difference as "differing," would immediately have revealed that there are many differences, and many ways of differing, as difference itself is indeed the principle of multiplicity and pluralization.

On this matter, Vattimo adopts a different stance. His evocation of the last part of *Sein und Zeit* and the question of why difference is—and ought not to be—forgotten shifts the discourse conspicuously. You could say that, through his critique of French neostructuralism, Vattimo succeeds not so much in *resolving* as in *repositioning* the question of difference. From his point of view, it is no longer a question of a purely descriptive remembering of the existence of a difference "as a matter of fact" (the simple fact that Being differs from beings), nor of the right stance to take with respect to this fact (for example, as Emanuele Severino suggests,[25] coming out resolutely in favor of Being). It is no longer even a question of the assumption of difference as a *methodological* and *metaphysical* principle (as we see in Deleuze, who not only aims, through Nietzsche, at a Leibnizian metaphysics of "singularities," but also defends difference as a sound methodological principle alternative to dialectic). The further step taken by Vattimo is this:

However, what is conventionally called "the philosophy of difference," grounded in Heidegger and prevalent today in a certain sector of French culture, tends to conceal and forget the various possible ways of problematizing difference. In general it fails, as I see it, to take onboard the suggestion made in the last section of Being and Time, *either in its narrow literal sense (why is difference forgotten?) or in its general methodological sense (what about difference as such?). It prefers instead to begin with the fact of the forgetting of difference, and to set against that a thought that strives instead to remember difference, rediscovering it and making it present to itself in various ways, and so claiming to position itself somehow beyond "metaphysics."*[26]

Here we see that in taking his distance from French "philosophy of difference," Vattimo is also pointing to a subtle ambiguity in Heidegger's ontological discourse, which remains the fulcrum of his interpretation of Heidegger: Is the forgetting of difference a "fact"? In what sense is it, and in what sense is it not? In other words, is it distinct from the world of ontically arrayed facts? In this regard, it is legitimate to suppose that Heideggerian ontology ought to achieve completion in some form of Hegelianism, more precisely in that form of Hegelianism rethought in linguistic terms that is hermeneutics for Vattimo.[27] The peculiarity of Vattimo's point of view, in this respect, is clearly revealed in "Dialectic and Difference," the last essay in *The Adventure of Difference*, where the "actuality" of Heidegger is measured by emphasizing the divergence between recalling (*ricordare*) as "*Er-innerung*" in Hegel and remembering (*rammemorazione*, literally "rememoration") as "*An-denken*" in Heidegger. The former, Vattimo notes, is an act of appropriation-interiorization, while the latter (albeit also grounded in a paradialectic nexus of memory and forgetting) is configured within an "event" which is the "death of God," and so cannot be appropriation because, elementarily, there is no individuated object or mnemonic datum to be (re)appropriated. Once again Vattimo takes his distance from neostructuralism: "We cannot speak of difference, in other words begin to surpass metaphysics, except by describing the conditions under which it comes to pass that it summons us peremptorily." [28]

The question is now put in its essential terms: *how* to speak of difference? Which means: how to speak of a possible transformation, meaning the emancipation of mankind from its own perverted humanism, and of philosophy from metaphysics (in the derogatory sense)? The French thinkers, who conceive the surpassing of metaphysics as the surpassing not only of the subject but also of historicity, end by talking about difference *forgetting that it has been forgotten*. In effect, difference is neither (just) the static and structural distinction between Being and beings (existent things) nor the functional divergence produced by thought. It is first and foremost:

> ...*temporal deferment or spacing-out. There is no thought of difference that is not remembering* (rammem-

orazione): *not just because difference is in fact forgotten by metaphysical thought, but also because difference is primarily deferment, is indeed the very temporal articulation of experience which has essentially to do with the fact of our mortality.*[29]

Evidently, it is not subjective historicity that is renounced by the Heideggerian sense of the relation between memory and forgetting. To avoid the twofold memory loss of French thinkers, it is thus essential to understand that the history of which we speak when we suggest recalling difference "is a history of messages," of calls and responses, but such that "the response never exhausts the call." Hence the transition to hermeneutics, meaning in this case the *dialogization* of ontology and history. Yet, notes Vattimo (in what is clearly the indication of a program), "the full implications of this hermeneutic modelling of history have not yet been clarified, either by Heidegger himself or by his interpreters and followers."[30] Even Derrida, who also stressed the temporality of difference, ultimately reduces the divergence to the simple evidence of historical *traces*, so in a way he promotes a re-ontification of temporality.

DIFFERENCE AND DIALECTIC

It was in this context, and with these premises, that weak thought came to seem a viable option. All the essays in the 1983 collection *Il pensiero debole*, planned and edited by Vattimo and Pier Aldo Rovatti, either touch on or deal directly with the destiny of dialectic and the themes of difference and/or dialectic. This indicates that the movement of weak thought concerns epistemology, as well as aesthetics, ethics, politics, and metaphilosophy, as dialectic and difference are formal principles that concern all these fields. But on a deeper level, as Vattimo's own essay in the book indicates, it designates a *metatheoretical* stance in the wide sense, an attempt to respond to the question: what orientation is imposed on thought, after the consummation of the dialectical horizon, which has dominated a wide swathe of European philosophy in the twentieth century?

The introduction coauthored by Vattimo and Rovatti traces a short history of twentieth-century dialectical and postdialectical philosophy, and describes the current status of the question. By the 1960s, the search for a new foundation had arrived at two tentative solutions, conflicting ones in certain respects. The first was the search for structures "free of any center or finality" ("subjectless"); the second was the search for a subjectivity "unsubstantial, more fluid, in course of becoming." It is not hard to see that they are referring to the structuralist and phenomenological traditions, respectively. By contrast, in the 1970s Vattimo and Rovatti see the emergence of a new negativity: structuralist theory and philosophies aspiring to a new subjectivity both turned out to be fundamentally "totalizing." "The tone of the debate changed, with the ongoing, albeit unwelcome, intrusion of a tragic [or] irrational element."[31] The upshot was reactionary or nostalgic theories about the "crisis of reason," and deconstructive and anarchic epistemologies.

The book avowedly takes this situation (a good fit with Nietzsche's theory of reactive-active nihilism) as its point of departure. But what exactly did Vattimo and Rovatti intend when they chose the term "weak"? For Rovatti,[32] it would appear, the prescription or indication contained in the formula refers primarily to the way a certain number of quite common logico-political and cognitive experiences lie *close to the limit*, and, so to speak, bleed into one another:

> *The subject diminishes while experience grows in bulk. Does the subject disappear? Or has the subject become so "small" that it is finally able to recognize itself in its own experience? Does experience multiply, grow confused, become illegible? Or has it filled itself with so many sounds that it can finally be heard?*[33]

Rovatti arrives at a definition of weak thought as a dialectic without synthesis, a thinking of the discrimination between two paths that never definitively opts for one or the other.[34] Umberto Eco's point of view is entirely different: he approaches the problem on the semantic and epistemological plane, and interprets weakness as connoting *pluralistic, scientifically prospectivistic.* For Eco the constitutive nucleus of a "weak" epistemology is a semantic model based on the figure of the labyrinth in its various formulations, especially that of the "encyclopedia." "Thought of the labyrinth and the encyclopedia is weak, inasmuch as conjectural and contextual, but reasonable because it allows an intersubjective control and leads neither to renunciation nor solipsism."[35]

Other authors in the collection (see particularly the article by Gianni Carchia) rightly redirect the entire problem back to the Hegelian question of mediation. If in Hegel, Carchia writes, "the *Zusammengehen* of subject and predicate *in* the copula" presents itself precisely as a new form of mediation that avoids the suppression of finiteness to which the philosophy of reflection leads, Heidegger's move consists in affirming the irreducibility of Being to the copula, in recognizing the *more,* the "unaware," that operates between subject and object. In this Heidegger is following Kant's lead, and it is the Kant of the theory of judgment, according to Carchia, who points the way toward resistance against the dialectical scheme, toward the premises for a "nonjudgmental, and therefore *logically weak*, thought."[36]

But what is the meaning of this emphasis on the "logical" that runs more or less explicitly through the essays in the collection? It's a fairly interesting question, I think, because one thing we can stipulate is that weak thought is and has been above all a response to the great limitative results of philosophical logic (in the sense of "logic of philosophy") after Kant, and between Kant and Hegel. In the text you are about to read, Vattimo indirectly puts this question right from the start in addressing the problem of the Kant-Hegel nexus. Now the tenor of these limitative results may also be described as specifically logical, given that the well-known results of Gödel and Tarski (the divergence of completeness and consistency, the necessity to distinguish between language and metalanguage) were actually anticipated in preformal terms precisely by Kant and Hegel. In the *Critique of Pure Reason,* Kant manifestly "discovers" the incompleteness of theoretical reason, and Hegel attempts to remedy this "discovery," or rather to make it the beginning of another way of proceeding in theoretical contexts (exactly like the so-called pioneers of recursivity). Hegel in this regard figures as the equivalent, in a philosophical and preformal setting, of Gödel and the recursivists.[37]

Vattimo's own essay for the volume is entitled "Dialettica, differenza, pensiero debole." In my view the most interesting aspect of the hypothesis he sets forth is that weak thought is defined on the basis of the categories of *totality* and *adequation*, characterizing both in such a way as to render them respectively comparable to the Gödelian concepts of *completeness* and *coherence*. It is important to note that in this essay the question is presented in a frankly metaphilosophical and logico-political perspective:

> *weak thought does not simply turn its back on dialectic and the thought of difference; rather they constitute a past for weak thought in the sense of the Heideggerian* Gewesenes, *with connotations of a sending and a destiny.*[38]

In a comment on Sartre's *Critique of Dialectical Reason*, Vattimo notes that dialectic is characterized by two principal notions: totality and reappropriation. He portrays both as metaphors or instances, respectively, of completeness, and descriptive conformity (or adequacy or correspondence). But considering that Vattimo's intellectual horizon is that of being-time-language, a continuum independent of any external referent, "descriptive conformity" amounts to the ontological equivalent of the notion of *coherence* (within an immanentistic horizon, coherence and correspondence are ultimately the same).

It is interesting to see how Vattimo deduces the debility of both principles from the failure of the dialectical program. The vacillation of the dialectical method is especially visible in Sartre when he demonstrates the "mythological" character of the Lukàcsian solution to the problem of totality—the imputation of a "total" vision to the proletariat, or more precisely to its intellectual vanguard, and to the party. In Adorno, Benjamin, and Bloch, the idea of totality is made to display its full range of ideological violence and falsity.

The importance and fascination of thinkers such as Benjamin, Adorno, and Bloch consists not so much in their having rethought dialectic, incorporating into it the critical exigences of micrology, as in their having valorized those exigencies even to the detriment of dialectic itself and of the very coherence and unity of their own thought. They are thinkers not of dialectic but of its dissolution.[39]

Benjamin perceives the violent and dogmatic nature of totalizing thought primarily in the way it blankets with silence all that might have come about but didn't, all that did not produce concrete, striking historical outcomes: the cult of historiography is eminently bourgeois, and dialectical effectualism (the real equals the rational) is its unmistakeable symptom. "From the elementary viewpoint of the living being, Adorno was right: wholeness is a falsehood"[40] (with an allusion to the way Lukàcs the revolutionary is deployed against Lukàcs the defender of totality in Benjamin and Adorno).

Still, Vattimo observes, the micrological instance defended by the enemies of totality gives way to the second problem, the question of reappropriation and the proper (coherence-consistency).[41] There is no guarantee that the "damned part," that which the dominant culture excludes, can in fact be uttered. Nothing assures us that, in attaining effectuality, the ineffectual does not also become the voice of domination and imposition. At this point there emerges the "thought of difference." Its similarity to negative and (post) dialectical Frankfurt thought is explicitly noted. From the vantage point of the philosophy of difference, in particular as elaborated by Heidegger, the critique of totality demands to be supplemented by a critique of appropriation (read: of *adequatio*, but also of descriptivity). Not only is the totalizing claim of metaphysical logic, and of dialectic itself, false and a vehicle of repression and violence; the critique of this claim must also address the unsustainability of the adequative and descriptive relation purportedly established between language (thought) and Being.

The critique of the claim to totality, in other words, must be combined with the critique of the confirmative-adequative claim to fix Being in terms of the presence of that which "there is." The adequative claims of critical-negative thought, its wish to be taken for a "better" version of dialectic should also be defeated. Vattimo here appears to read Heidegger's intimation about the temporalization of the a priori, and his reflection on the relation of Being and language, as a response to the need to "open up" logic as ontology (the question of the "uttering" of Being).

Now it is this aspect that determines the key difference between weak thought (in this variant) and any logical weakening whatever of procedures and principles (in fact, any discovery of paradoxes and limitations in the domain of logic translates, or may effectively translate, into a weakening of language of some kind). The difference between ontological weakening (in the Heideggerian sense) and any other logical weakening may then be formulated as follows: 1. Weak thought does not aim to avoid contradiction, but lies in the recurrence of contradiction, in its constitutive self-presentation as a structural requisite of the language of Being.[42] 2. Weak thought is also the idea of a suprapersonal destiny of the logos which disallows any logical *decision*. This second aspect is especially telling: if this thesis is true, strictly speaking one could not even *decide* in favor of contradiction, and this is what distinguishes weak thought from any logic whatsoever, even of a "paraconsistent" or in general "nonclassical" kind.

Moreover, since the point at issue concerns the modalities of discourse and thought, it is clear that the Heideggerian thesis retroacts on itself, that it presents itself as a proposal for the overcoming of metaphysics and dialectic that also proposes a new way of understanding the very notion of "overcoming."

NIHILISM, HERMENEUTICS, AND POSTMODERNITY

The problem of the prefix *Über-* is the dominant motif of Vattimo's thought in his engagement with Nietzsche, Heidegger, the French thinkers, and the dialectical tradition, as it evolves in the 1970s and the early 1980s. It was during these years that the solution grew expansive and comprehensible in all its details. The essays in the 1985 volume *The End of Modernity*[43] make especially clear the way in which the surpassing of metaphysics (and the subject) is undertaken by Vattimo with what Berti calls "greater coherence" in comparison to the French thinkers. And it is this coherence that drives weak thought toward that particular asymptotic dialectic ("vertiginous" logic, he calls it) that remains the "strong" core of Vattimo's work. The first essay, entitled "An Apology for Nihilism," highlights the fundamental impasse of twentieth-century thought with respect to nihilism:

> *Phenomenology and early existentialism, together with humanistic Marxism and the theorization of the "sciences of the spirit," are manifestations of the same strand of thought, one that binds together a large sector of European culture. It could be characterized by its "pathos of authenticity," what Nietzsche would call its resistance to the accomplishment of nihilism.*[44]

Not even what Vattimo calls the Wittgensteinian "mystical," and which (quite singularly) he views as expressed in the theory of "local" truths, escapes the pathos of authenticity.

> *To the devaluation of the highest values and the death of God, the only reaction—examples abound—is the (pathetic and metaphysical) defence of other, "truer" values, for example, those of marginal or popular cultures as opposed to the values of dominant cultures, the subversion of literary or artistic canons, and so on.*[45]

Vattimo, we observe, assimilates French differentialism to any other antinihilistic "reaction." In the technological world, which Vattimo views as the world of nihilism, there simply is no theory or philosophical thesis—not even differentialism or the metaphysics of "singularities" and "simulacra"—that succeeds in accounting "more authentically" for experience, "because authenticity—the proper, reappropriation—has itself subsided with the death of God."[46]

The Heideggerian concept of *Verwindung* becomes, then, the key term for the whole theory of surpassing, and a preliminary indication for a contemporary practice of philosophy that could succeed in operating under conditions of the loss of "the proper" and of "totality." But it was the theory of postmodernity, especially as formulated by Lyotard (perhaps the most philosophically significant statement of postmodernism, along with that of Hassan), that now offered Vattimo an ideal terrain on which to frame the discourse on difference, nihilism, dialectic (and weak thought), and definitively valorize this idea of a *weak* difference ("weak" in the sense of *verwunden*) as a good alternative to dialectic.

Lyotard defines postmodernity in terms not very remote from those sketched by Vattimo in the essay in *Il Pensiero Debole*: as the collapse of the *grands récits* (overarching narratives), and of the local principles of conformity and adequacy.[47] In the postmodern age everything plays out and comes about in terms of performativity: exactly as in the world of nihilism, in which Being is reduced to exchange value. So one sees how well the theory fits the theses that Vattimo had formulated and was continuing to formulate in those years.[48] If "modern" is the Cartesian foundation, "postmodernism" is nihilism in the sense of mankind "rolling from the center toward X."[49] But postmodernism is also Heideggerian re-memorative thought, which captures difference beyond the claimed objectivations and decisions of the subject (this connection is, among other things, one of the reasons Vattimo discerns a certain consonance between nihilism and the thought of the late Heidegger, detecting in Heidegger "a nihilist tone"). If modern equals "metaphysical," if it equals the latest "name," the latest version of metaphysics, then postmodern equals postmetaphysical, but on the basis of that mode of surpassing that, as Heidegger says, is in reality not the elimination but the "repetition" of metaphysics. If the "modern" is "objectivating" thought, claiming to describe "stable structures of being," postmodernism is pre-eminently thought that doesn't make that claim.

However, in virtue of the same principle by which, as Nietzsche says, "all is interpretation" is also an interpretation, the surpassing indicated by the prefix "post-" is of a special kind. As Vattimo puts it in "Nihilism and the Postmodern in Philosophy," the final essay in *The End of Modernity*: "[*Verwindung*] is nothing like dialectical *Aufhebung*, or the way we 'turn our backs' on a past that no longer concerns us. Precisely this difference between *Verwindung* and *Überwindung* can help us to define in philosophical terms the 'post-' in 'post-modernism'."[50]

VERWINDUNG

It should be recalled that the problem of difference, like the problem of dialectic, is ultimately a problem of "passage": a problem of critical distance-taking from the past, but also a problem of logico-theoretical and ontological distinction (of the difference between Being and beings, or of differing in general). Vattimo explains that this problem was resolved by Nietzsche in a way that anticipates the meaning of Heidegger's theory of *Verwindung*, and the "post-" in "postmodernism." In *Human, All Too Human* the question of how to break free of the historical malady, or more precisely, "how to get free of modernity," "is posed in a new way" by Nietzsche: "*Human, All Too Human* operates a genuine dissolution of modernity through a radicalization of its own constitutive tendencies."[51] So what we have is a dissolution-surpassing that is primarily acceptance and radicalization.

Quite clearly, this attitude is justified by the fact that modernity itself is essentially the age of surpassing/overtaking, and so to surpass it means to actualize it, reconfirm it performatively. Modernity is the age of "the new that ages," of a whirlwind of novelties each overtaking the last, "in a movement that discourages all creativity even as it demands creativity, and imposes it as the only form of life." So obviously "no way out of modernity can possibly be found in terms of an overcoming of it," and "another way must be found."[52]

The "other way" suggested by Vattimo is a peculiar declension of the concept of *Verwindung* in a Nietzschean key. It is evident that *Verwindung* is both a semantic and pragmatic principle.[53] It indicates how the categories of classical metaphysics are to be *understood* and *used*. At the same time it is an ethico-pragmatic and methodological principle, in the sense that it indicates the attitude to adopt in the face of the decline of metaphysics. *Verwindung* appears, moreover, to be a dialectical notion, but with a few salient differences. It is characterized by two terms: "remission to" in the sense of "entrusting oneself to" and "remission from" in the sense of "recovering from" a disease. It bears the connotations of declining-twisting apart, overcoming-distortion, repetition-intensification, and so on. In "Dialettica, differenza, pensiero debole," Vattimo writes:

> the Heideggerian surpassing of metaphysics may look like a dialectical overcoming [Überwindung], but it thinks differently just because it is a Verwindung; yet as such it also prosecutes something proper to dialectic.[54]

So we observe the idiomatic speculative effect of the notion of *Verwindung*: it speaks the prosecution-twisting apart of modernity, and at the same time performs that which it speaks and describes. So the notion of *Verwindung* is not just a critique of metaphysical descriptivity, it also exhibits an alternative form of description. *Verwindung* describes the movement of Being as *Überlieferung* and *Ge-schick*, and is at the same time "the mode in which thought thinks the truth of Being understood as *Überlieferung* and *Ge-schick*."[55]

This also leads to a structural variation in the type of duality that characterizes the semantics of *Verwindung* with respect to the semantic duality of dialectical notions. Here the second meaning, that which is simultaneously implied along with the primary signified, is not simply the opposite but the different in the temporal and spatial (or structural) sense. Hence the oblique relation that is established between the terms in play: *distorsion* is certainly not the opposite of *prosecution*, rather it indicates a modality of prosecution. "Remission to" in turn indicates a modality of "remission from": to recover from an illness, but with an attitude of abandon, not violent opposition, without trying to halt the course of the malady by resisting it. In this sense *Verwindung* may also be seen as a reinterpretation of *Aufhebung*, but corrected in the direction of the historical empiricism that is typical of hermeneutics.

In *Beyond Interpretation* (1994)[56] the nihilistic orientation imparted to hermeneutics by Vattimo assumes a characteristically circular, reflexive, and more properly *speculative* nature. Circularity here plays a methodological as well as a thematic role. The point of departure is a historico-epochal thesis, which soon finds itself outstripped by a metatheoretical commitment. Nihilism is the vicissitude of western ontology, the trajectory of the gradual growing lighter/emptying out of the traditional philosophical categories, and the progressive weakening of the Aristotelian notion of Being. The stance corresponding to this factual condition (the verification of which is overtly historical-interpretative) is that kind of affirmative nihilism that defines the assimilation between *Verwindung* and the "post-" in "post-modernism." So there is a matter of fact, given by the progressive "self-consummation" of Being (to use Vattimo's expression); and there is a consequent behavior, the lightening of the traditional categories, the weakening of thought. Note, however, that the second aspect is reflexive and retroactive, in other words it brings significant variations in meaning to the first. In fact the weakening of theoretical discourse is also and primarily, as we have seen, an attenuation of the descriptive nexus between philosophical language and states of affairs, hence the descriptive premises from which the discourse proceeds:

- cannot be configured as if they were premises in the pre-Hegelian sense of the term

- cannot be evaluated as if they were a theory or a *Weltanschauung*, a position staked out regarding the structure of the world.

ARGUMENTATION AND PROVENANCE

This solution (or rather acceptance) of the antinomy of modern reason shows itself far from "irrational" when we turn to the attempt to delineate the principles of hermeneutic argumentation that Vattimo briefly undertook in a 1993 essay, "The Right to Argument."[57] Two essential data emerge: philosophy's right still to be, albeit in changed circumstances, discourse on (the) *totality*, and the link between *argumentation* and *provenance*.

The right that philosophy asserts vis-à-vis totality, Vattimo says, cannot be framed as a right to the "expression" of a *Weltanschauung*, nor propose itself as arbitrary "creation."[58] Yet it must arise in a relation of fidelity or consequentiality with respect to something: and in fact no *first* philosophy is really that, since any posing of a problem or formulation of a question is the fruit "of answers received, inherited, already available," and on the same basis no philosophy can (as science can in certain cases) "pronounce conclusively (i. e., experimentally)" (which simply means: there is no absolute beginning or absolute termination of discourse).[59]

As a tentative response to questions "received, inherited, already available," every theory, every "argumentative enterprise," is based on an array of heterogeneous presuppositions, and so is constitutively "impure."[60] A variety of questions and answers come to us from the past, and our interpretation of them, as well as the selective choice of which of them to answer, are "ordinative" and constitutive. The task of interpretation is ultimately to order and put into dialogue (or put itself into dialogue with) that which our tradition hands down.[61] But since what we have available is provenance, the same a priori of which we make use is "provenient" and therefore cannot be fixed once and for all, nor portrayed descriptively (the a priori elements of knowledge "are inscribed in natural language—profoundly marked by historicity—into which the *Dasein* is thrown time and again").[62] So there is no given order of the a priori of which we make use in interpreting provenance. The peculiar work of philosophy, if it is to keep faith with the endless coming-about of tradition, is thus not objectivation, but reversion to the "eventual" conditions that anticipate any objectivation and "open" the conditions of truth.[63] Finally: both the form and the content of this reversion are the fruit of participatory and dialogic work; the criteria of the deconstruction and reordering of the past are themselves found in participatory and dialogic terms.

The relation between argumentation and provenance then arises out of what Gadamer calls "a hermeneutically educated consciousness": the only way we can argue is to take into account the paths already trodden historically; more specifically, history teaches us the ways down which "we must no longer go." We can only argue if we recognize that argumentation belongs to a tissue of opinions and conventions already operating beneath our awareness, and only if we ask ourselves what the times "require" (and avoid offering them what they already have more than enough of). Finally, we cannot argue exclusively on the arbitrary basis of predilections, or even on the basis of what seems to be simply evident (hence the extramethodological and at the same time selective nature of this point of view).

The singular aspect of the whole approach, however, is that this apparent "urbanization" of Heideggerian ontology is defended as logically and historically necessary. The opening of philosophical discourse to historico-pragmatic, political, and social implications is (appears here to be) the response to a request implicit in the very "opening" of traditional ontology sought by Heidegger. The question of totality here becomes, inevitably, the heeding of totality.

For Hegel the preliminary totality, philosophy's universe of reference, is the contradictory totality, inclusive of Being and non-Being (the "Boolean" world defined by the principle "X and not-X together exhaust the universe"). For Heidegger and Jaspers it is the omnicomprehensive horizon of Being, inclusive of human life and its specific paradoxical structure. For this hermeneutic ontology, the totality to which philosophy refers is an open domain, not pre-describable, in which history, and language, and the various cultural contaminations of both, supply the *pensandum*, the material for thought to work. The universe of reference is no longer only the commixture of Being and thought, ideal and real, affirmation and negation, etc., nor is it only the structure of existence in the paradoxical form described by Kierkegaard and inherited by existentialism; it is a heterogeneous entity, a multiform and fundamentally "discrete" totality which Vattimo identifies in the Being-history-language of hermeneutic effectuality.

The two questions that arise at this point predictably concern the normativity and identifiability of provenance. In what sense can we operate selectively on provenance? In other words: which voices from the tradition should be heeded and which discarded? Furthermore: who can decide whether the "response" to tradition is authentic, or just an arbitrary construct? In the face of these questions, the Heideggerian-hermeneutic solution consists in pointing to the extramethodological nature of interpretation. The very theory of provenance entails the hermeneutic assumption that theory never completely dominates that with which it thematically and methodically deals. In other words, the burden of metatheoretical and methodological decision is transferred to the object: it is actually the theme that decides the nature of the method; it is the choice of Being that determines the heterogeneity and impurity of the historico-existential foundation, and the particular dialectic-without-synthesis that weak thought unfurls. Just as, in Hegel, it was ultimately the idea of the world of the spirit as bivalent totality (the idea of totality as a concrete synthesis of affirmation and negation, subjective and objective, finite and infinite, etc.) that determined the choice of dialectic as the methodology of thought, likewise it is the thematic choice of Being as heterogeneous totality that determines the methodology of provenance, and participation.

THIS BOOK

Vattimo is certainly one of the "philosophers of technology," which is to say the thinkers who have tried to understand contemporaneity in its technical-scientific development, neither condemning it nor condemning its outcomes, but as he would put it, "heeding its call." His work along these lines can today be described as accomplished with *Beyond Interpretation*, which is the last firmly and unequivocally "philosophical" book he has written. Subsequently, with *Belief in Belief* (1996),[64] Vattimo set off down an entirely new path, which has led him to a profoundly different kind of philosophical militancy. His style has grown much simpler, losing many links with technicalities and references to the philosophical tradition that once characterized it.

It is important to emphasize—and the book you are about to read will confirm it—that this turn has not, properly speaking, been a form of reactive compensation, or a detachment from philosophy, but the fulfillment of a certain process: the natural fulfillment, as I see it, of a process typical of a certain kind of philosophy, the one practiced by Vattimo, which can legitimately be called (the name brings to mind the time when Marxism was in bloom) "concrete theory."

Moving into politics (or "taking a dive" into politics, as he ironically puts it here), Vattimo has simply developed one of the facets of the speculativity (reflexivity, or commixture of interpretativity and praxis) which is proper to the categories of his thought, and which in it constitutes an original reinterpretation both of the Hegelian dialectic and of the postdialectical speculativity of the second Heidegger. So there is a philosophical necessity or *fate* (just as, notes Vattimo, there is a "logic" to the semantic slippages and fugues to which nihilism subjects the categories of classical metaphysics) expressed in this apparent shift to the "ontic," and the pages that follow supply many suggestions, I believe, for understanding this necessity.

The discourse unfolds in three movements. Vattimo initially makes clear the reasons why his vision of philosophical practice, while distancing itself from science, does not seek any assimilation to literature, sociology, the sciences of culture, or any form of artistic-literary arbitrariness. What I see as important in Vattimo's work is this clear vision of philosophy as something apart from the sciences (formal as well as natural), and from the humanities and art: but "apart" precisely inasmuch as profoundly compromised in the fundamental problematics of all of them, and bound by a thousand links of affinity and overlap with every cultural practice.

Secondly, Vattimo here specifies his interpretation of the concept of truth. If for Aristotle one must choose truth or friendship, here we clearly see a preference for friendship, but grounded in the belief that the philosophical theory of truth cannot break the ancient link with the *polis*, the terrain from which it grew and to which it speaks. So Vattimo speaks of "fidelity" (rather than descriptive adequacy) to Being as event, and of a subject that is above all dialogue (or as I have called it: participation).

This does not in the least entail a move away from logic and toward rhetoric, nor is this an irresponsible choice in terms of its theoretical and historical motivations. In a recent text entitled "Les raisons que la raison ne connaît pas" ("the reasons that reason knows not"),[65] Vattimo develops the question, showing (once again) how the defense of the "reasons of the heart" is well undergirded in his case by intense intellectual labor. Many contemporary European thinkers actually agree on the relative dominance of friendship or *pietas* over truth (meaning the putative adequacy of thing and discourse); so does Christianity in a "Dostoyevskyan" mode. Levinas emphasizes respect for the "other," Habermas emphasizes Hegel's youthful doctrine of love and the communicative practices of the lifeworld. But as Vattimo sees it, only a precise ontological choice can prevent these stances from sliding into some form of surreptitious dogmatism, obliquely transforming "the other" into the transcendent "Other" in the case of Levinas, or obliquely reaffirming an absolute reason through the imperative of absolute communicative transparency in that of Habermas. This ontological choice, as we have seen, privileges Being as event, privileges the "eventuality" of Being. It is thus evident, and these pages confirm it, that Vattimo thinks of friendship (of participation, of the *metekein* to which Gadamer assigns the foundational task of theory) as precisely the ambit in which the "paradoxes of truth" always find, again and again, realization and solution. Note the subtle but decisive variation with respect to the primacy of practical reason: here we have the primacy of *participative* reason.[66]

In the final section of the present text, on the responsibility, vocation, and destiny of philosophy, Vattimo supplies us with a clue for understanding how much the tensions in contemporary philosophical practice (between historians and theorists, between journalist-philosophers and professor-philosophers, between philosophical specialization and the philosopher's mission as "functionary of humanity") are in his eyes both comprehensible and completely "lived-out" by a philosophy that assumes the burden of its own finiteness, and elaborates this same finiteness politically (as emancipation) and religiously (as redemption). These pages conclude with what could be called (if the irony of weak thought allowed it) a theory of the religious-political-historical sublime, meaning the disproportion and, at the same time, familiarity that the viewpoint of the *polis* always imposes on thought. It would seem that one cannot be fully a philosopher, according to Vattimo, except by continuously confronting the vision not of totality (whether understood in the ontological or logical sense, in the political or the religious sense), but how far we are from totality. But in this sense everyone ought to be able to call themselves, and able to be, "philosophers." Everyone should have this privilege of "seeing themselves" in their own limits: a privilege that is, says Vattimo, typically "European."

POSTSCRIPT (2009)

The essay here presented was written around ten years ago. It is not outdated, actually, because the theoretical bases of Vattimo's philosophical work were already clear at that time. The aim of the essay was to present these bases in a synthetic and comprehensive way, locating them within the horizon of continental philosophy in the last three decades of the twentieth century. However, a few further words are now in order, mainly referring to developments in Vattimo's philosophical program. So in what follows I will briefly summarize the path I traced, and then consider some recent acquisitions of Vattimo's philosophy.[67]

Nietzsche and Nihilism

After a preliminary specification of the meaning of "weak" in the expression "weak thought" (to which I will return below) the essay lays out Vattimo's trajectory, beginning with the interpretation of Nietzsche he presented in *Il soggetto e la maschera* (1971) and other writings. This interpretation brought Vattimo's philosophy into systematic confrontation with French neostructuralism, namely with Gilles Deleuze, Jean-François Lyotard, Michel Foucault, and Jacques Derrida. Vattimo shares Deleuze's and Lyotard's affirmative interpretation of Nietzschean *nihilism*[68]: nihilism is not simply the shared acknowledgment of the end of all values ("all extreme values lose their value"), but rather the condition of science "that dances with light feet," and the age of philosophers able to accept "the dangerous maybe." However, Vattimo does not share Deleuze's and Lyotard's vitalism, and offers instead a Heideggerian and hermeneutical interpretation of the theory.

Difference

In this interpretation Heidegger's notion of *difference* plays a central role, as we see in *The Adventure of Difference* (1980) and his writings from around the end of the 1970s. Like Derrida, and Deleuze as well, Vattimo refuses the too strictly ontological conception of difference (between Being and beings) posited by Heidegger, and adopts an idea of *difference* in the sense of *differing*, that is to say, the operation of keeping one's distance from traditional metaphysics, with its rigid conception of Being. He also stresses, like

Derrida, the *temporal* nature of differing: difference is actually deferment, postponement. But unlike Deleuze and Derrida, Vattimo points out that, as Heidegger rightly maintained, difference has been *forgotten*: we have lost the static difference between Being and beings, as well as the dynamic differing of Being from itself. Consequently, what we have lost is the very possibility of acting against this oblivion, the very possibility of constructing some alternative vision of Being that we might set against the traditional metaphysical vision. Finally: we have lost the very possibility of political action against the oppressive system grounded in that traditional vision.

Verwindung and Postmodernism

Heidegger's conception of *Verwindung* is adopted by Vattimo to solve the problem. The concept involves a specific idea of "overcoming plus distortion," leave-taking, and preserving. It is similar in a way to Hegel's notion of *Aufhebung*, but it also bears the connotation of "recovery from a disease." So we have to *verwunden* metaphysics: maintaining it, at the same time "healing over" its structural oblivion of Being and difference. This idea finds a specific application in the interpretation of the meaning of the "post-" in "postmodernism." Vattimo's interpretation of postmodernism, as presented in *The End of Modernity* (1985), is in fact a confrontation with Lyotard's diagnosis of *The Postmodern Condition* from the perspective of the Heidegger-Nietzsche nexus from which his own philosophy emerged. More specifically, the notion of *Verwindung* is employed by Vattimo to express the idea of overcoming implicit in the concept of postmodernism. "Precisely this difference between *Verwindung* and *Überwindung* can help us to define in philosophical terms the term 'post-modernism'."[69]

Dialectic

Vattimo's use of the notion of *Verwindung* also represents a definite stance in relation to the conception of dialectic developed in the so-called western Marxism of Bloch, Adorno, Benjamin, Marcuse, and Horkheimer. This is evident in the essay "Dialettica, differenza e pensiero debole" (1983), where Vattimo clearly explains that weak thought originates in the failure of the dialectical program. He stresses that the program failed because of the ambition of "totality and reappropriation" that drove it. In this sense the importance of thinkers like Benjamin or Adorno lies in their destruction of the totalizing-appropriative nature of dialectical thought, which could have supplied the philosophical premises for an *antitotalitarian communism*, something which was systematically devalued by the effective applications of Marxism.

Thus the path is traced: the structural bases of Vattimo's thought are broadly these. What needs to be added, and indeed was already evident in the whole development, is first the *metaphilosophical* inspiration of Vattimo's stance, then the *political* outcome of these premises.

Metaphilosophy

As to Vattimo's metaphilosophical commitment, something has been already suggested, in section 7 above, about the combination of "argumentation and provenance" proposed by Vattimo as a cipher of hermeneutic philosophy.

The commitment to both clarity and historical awareness is exactly the reason why Vattimo then considered a possible combination of analytic and continental philosophy within a weak, hermeneutical horizon. Analytic philosophy is in fact renowned for its attention to argumentation, and continental philosophy (especially the Italian strain) is characterized by attention to history. Karl Otto Apel, Ernst Tugendhat, and Richard Rorty have, at different times and in different ways, been the best-known bridge builders between the two traditions. In particular, Vattimo has established a dialogue with Rorty, who in that period was close to Gadamer's hermeneutics. There are some differences between Rorty's and Vattimo's perspectives,[70] but perhaps the main point concerns the idea of philosophy. In the polemical climate of the years around the beginning of the new millennium, and specifically in the controversies about the "drift" of postmodernism and poststructuralism, Rorty focused on the opposition of realism and antirealism, or as he put it: the opposition between *fuzzies* and *techies*. Vattimo's main concern in the discussion has instead been the metaphilosophical question. "After distinction and contrast, this is the time of recollection and global reconsideration," Vattimo wrote,[71] and the aim was to combine analytical attention to argumentation with continental awareness regarding history.

So what basically distinguishes Vattimo's point of view from Rorty's is precisely the former's attention to the destiny of philosophy, especially in the public sphere. Vattimo does not seem to share the condemnation of "philosophy" by Rorty and Heidegger as being "antidemocratic" (Rorty) or "objectifying" (Heidegger). But in what sense, and on what grounds, should a comprehensive notion of philosophy be retained, overriding the distinction between analytic and continental philosophy? Is Vattimo's only an *irenic* attitude, to be set against the *ironic* attitude, defended by Rorty? Vattimo's answer is here for the reader to find in the pages of *The Responsibility of the Philosopher*, and has become more and more relevant in subsequent years, involving the public, political destiny of philosophical discourse.

Politics

In a recent essay on "The Political Outcome of Hermeneutics,"[72] Vattimo defends the idea of the fundamentally political vocation of hermeneutics. This specific political bent—so Vattimo thinks—is already evident in Gadamer's conception of the primacy of art in the experience of truth (though Gadamer's philosophy was strictly nonpolitical, and Gadamer's political attitude was rather conservative). Benjamin, Marcuse, and Adorno specifically gave a political sense to the "aesthetization of experience" typical of the world contemporary to them (not to be confused—thus Benjamin—with the "aesthetization of politics" evident in totalitarian fascist regimes). And in this combination of aesthetics and politics we find the most authentic inspiration of hermeneutic philosophy.

The intuition of the ultimately political commitment of hermeneutics is especially important nowadays, in Vattimo's view. Specifically, two aspects of public debate are now to be hermeneutically viewed and treated. The first "consists of bioethical and environmental problems, which concern the public relevance of science, and religion." The second involves "the multicultural society in which we live." Both multiculturalism and biopolitical problems, in Vattimo's view, call for a hermeneutic approach to politics. (The reader should bear in mind that in Italy the public sphere is occupied almost daily by both bioethical controversies and debates about immigration.)

But of what should this approach specifically consist? What is the specific import of hermeneutics in the debate about these delicate and controversial topics?

Two terms should be carefully taken into consideration: the first is *metaphysics*, and the second is *truth*. As regards the first, it should be noted that Vattimo's thought belongs to a tradition in which the term *metaphysics* does not simply denote a philosophical discipline, that is the attempt to inquire into the nature of Being and beings, but rather the dogmatic (wrong) version of this same discipline. "Metaphysics," in Heidegger's view is the realistic, descriptive orientation of science, involving the dogmatic claim to capture reality in its proper nature. In Heideggerian terms, this methodological realism is based on an implicit oblivion of Being (of the difference between Being and beings), which ultimately expresses itself in the nihilism and subjectivism of modernity. As we have seen, Vattimo does not totally endorse Heidegger's negative attitude toward nihilism: his idea is rather that there is a progressive lightening (a growing lighter) of Being in history, and this is not bad in itself, as it works as a guarantee of freedom.[73]

The weak conception of Being (typically expressed by Gadamer's hermeneutics) is seen as an alternative to metaphysics (in the derogatory sense). And it can profitably be applied in contemporary discussions about life and human beings (euthanasia, abortion, stem cells). The basic insight is that, as we ultimately do not know the exact point at which a person begins being (or stops being) a person, any attempt to impose an idea of "human life" meant to guide the drafting of legal statutes in this regard is dogmatic, antidemocratic, and basically antiphilosophical in principle.

The idea of "bioethics without metaphysics" advanced by Vattimo in *La vita dell'altro. Bioetica senza metafisica* (2006)[74] is not to be confused with the idea of *Ethics Without Ontology* defended by Hilary Putnam[75] in his book of that title: there is no drive to minimize or criticize ontology in Vattimo's stance (and in general hermeneutic philosophy, in all its versions, has always presented itself as an *ontological* perspective). Rather, there is the attempt to save *philosophical* ontology, by distinguishing it from *scientific* and *religious* ontologies. It is the philosophical perspective, with its specifically nihilistic (free, non-dogmatic) attitude, that can usefully deal with ontological discussions in the public sphere.[76]

As to the notion of truth, Vattimo has recently produced a book on the subject, summarizing his ideas as developed over thirty years: *Addio alla verità* (2009; Farewell to Truth).[77] In Vattimo's conception of politics, we may say that there is a sort of *mobilization* of truth. The point is basically that even though there are many truths about which we haven't significant doubts (say: "$2 + 2 = 4$," "Napoleon died on St. Elena," and so on), in controversial contexts truth tends to fade away. Any appeal to truth in such contexts is doomed to incur the charge of dogmatism (which is to say, in his terms: metaphysics). (In this sense, Vattimo's criticism of truth is perfectly consistent with the tradition of scepticism in its mature version, the one elaborated in the synthesis of Sextus Empiricus.) But the point is that these controversial contexts are the only politically relevant ones, and the only ones that truly call into question the notion of truth. So the philosophical-political attitude toward truth ought to be characterized by a sort of methodical nihilism: a philosopher should systematically *mobilize* truth, in critical contexts.

We can see then that *Addio alla verità* does not properly suggest some effective refusal of truth, but rather presents a theory of truth, in which a singular form of coherentism based on the Christian principle of *agape* is combined with radical scepticism (or rather methodical nihilism).[78] We can also see how this attitude toward truth may profitably be applied when we come to deal with problems of immigration and multiculturalism. The point is that in controversial contexts (the ones in which truth is really relevant) there is no possible search for truth if we are not interested in a strong form of agreement that is to be identified as *friendship*. Metaphysical truth is based on a vision of the world that will turn into dogma in these contexts. Logical truth is based on constructed *domains* or *worlds*, which will be useless in controversial situations in which the construct itself is at issue. Properly philosophical-hermeneutic truth instead is concerned with truthful/friendly ways of constructing these visions, domains, or worlds. And it is this constructing which is at stake in multicultural contexts. In this sense, there is in fact a primacy of friendship over truth: not because the former should substitute for the latter, but because the latter is politically grounded in the former.

Exactly this idea is the philosophical premise at the basis of Vattimo's antitotalitarian communism (see *Ecce Comu*, 2007).[79] And it involves, as I have tried to show, a complex revision of the dialectical (logical) and metaphysical (ontological) bases of philosophical discourse, especially when assumed in its political, public, applications. At the basis of it is the idea of the third-level awareness mentioned in section one: "everything is interpretation, and this is an interpretation too, and we should not forget this fundamental frailty (weakness) of truth." Here we also find a close connection to Hannah Arendt's idea of moral responsibility in controversial political contexts.[80] Arendt repeatedly stressed, in fact, that "respectable people" generally did not oppose Nazism and fascism, whereas marginal, nonsocially integrated people refused the "alignment" without hesitation. Being without faith and values, being free of societal bonds, is thus a good premise for truth in morally controversial contexts. One might posit that in those cases, while Heidegger asserted that "only a God can save us," it may be nihilism, instead, that will lead us to salvation.[81]

1 | PHILOSOPHY AND SCIENCE

There are a few things I wish to make clear at the outset. The first is that I do not regard philosophy as a handmaiden to science; indeed, I do not believe there is a privileged rapport between philosophy and any part of the scientific spectrum—not the exact sciences, not the natural sciences, not the "sciences of the spirit" (the *Geisteswissenschaften*—the humanities and social sciences). Indeed, I do not believe that philosophy is a science at all if we are using the word strictly in accord with its prevalent modern connotation. If by science is meant any form of knowledge,[1] then it is obvious that you have to know a few things to do philosophy, but if science is used to mean a form of knowledge equipped with fixed methods, cumulative results, and repeatable experiments, and above all with set guidelines and an institutional framework, then I very much doubt that philosophy is anything like science. You might be able to call the history of philosophy a science, because like the history of anything else it contains more or less objective points of reference: if someone publishes a book on the thought of Kant, you can check to see whether or not he has done his homework, if he knows the texts for example, and has mastered the secondary literature. But by the time Kant came to write the *Critique of Pure Reason*, it was already difficult to determine if this was "science" or not, and in any case it seems to me that, as far as Kant was concerned, the scientific imperative meant that it was imperative to have a criterion, a definition that would demarcate that which was "scientific" from that which was not.

Many would likely assent to the view that philosophy is not a science; it is the status of philosophy as a university discipline that causes problems. Naturally it suits us, because otherwise who would pay our salaries, but at bottom there always remains some uncertainty, a gray area. Philosophy may be a university discipline, but it can't be treated as if it were a cumulative, experimental, objective form of knowledge. The question therefore arises: if it is not a science, or even a cumulative and progressive form of knowledge with objective data that can be checked, what is it?

Let's go back to square one: why is it not a science? Aristotle held that it was; metaphysics was knowledge of Being as such and topped the hierarchy of the sciences, followed by knowledge of Being as quantity and Being as motility: philosophy, mathematics, and physics. What has happened since? Why is this Aristotelian outlook no longer defensible? Here there is a problem of content, inasmuch as physics is no longer definable as the science of movement, or mathematics as the science of quantity. But from the formal point of view as well, the history of philosophy shows that many facets of what was once regarded holistically as knowledge have been *positivized* and split off as specific knowledges about various sectors of reality. As for knowledge of Being in and of itself, it has become increasingly refractory to classification as a science, especially since Kant.

After Kant, science was formalized very strictly in modern terms, as a system of propositions that presuppose sensory verifiability: if you cannot bind concepts to sensory data, you do not have real science. And that is how philosophy sank to relatively ancillary status with respect to science. Many still speak of Kantian philosophy as a theory of knowledge that studies the conditions of possibility of the sciences, as what we can call a second-order science. But if that is true, I would stipulate nevertheless that it is still a science critiquing science, an exploration of its conditions of possibility and its limits. As for what Kant calls metaphysics, it is no accident that the attempt to endow metaphysics with a scientific dimension coincides with a profound crisis of metaphysics: from the late-nineteenth-century neo-Kantians on, it becomes evident that transcendental philosophy is a critique and an overcoming of metaphysics. All that remains of metaphysics is the description of the a priori structures of reason, and this is the perspective, as I see it, that passes over with a few variations into the regional ontologies of Husserl.

In any case, with Kant it is no longer possible for philosophy to be the science of Being in and of itself. And that holds good for all that follows from Kant, apart from idealism. German idealism could be defined as the last great effort to link the Aristotelian signification to the Kantian one: Hegel would not say that either Kant or Aristotle was wrong, he would say that the theory of the a priori forms is also the theory of Being. After Hegel, though, the question starts to become murky. I have the impression that in nineteenth- and twentieth-century thought, Kantism rather than Hegelism was the main target of criticism. The very thinkers who criticized Hegel from a Kantian perspective, from Cohen and Windelband to Dilthey and others, actually wound up rehearsing Hegelian solutions. The claim to ground the various knowledges in a more or less subjective form of phenomenalism (the most obscure and controverted point of the transcendental philosophies) is not in the least a Hegelian claim, it's only in Kant, or more properly in the use of Kant to ground a theory of science, for metascientific and encyclopedic ends—Kant as deployed by neo-Kantians. Indeed, in Hegel we already have an attempt to modify this claim, with the theory of the Spirit as suprapersonal historical instance, and the whole of knowledge as an effective historical subject.

To be schematic, what no longer functions after Kant (what is failing to function in the unfolding of neo-Kantism) is the idea that there exists a stable and universal reason. Kantism is battered by cultural anthropology, by the plurality of cultures, and even, I would hazard, by the objections Nietzsche raises to Kant, and by what emerges with positivism. Hegel is not the main target. What batters Hegel is Kierkegaard, existentialism, and the Kierkegaard renaissance of the twentieth century; but even Kierkegaard's objections are always tip-toeing delicately along a crest, always on the point of "toppling" back into the history of Spirit (as a moment, at least, of the dialectic of absolute knowledge).

All this merely confirms that philosophy can no longer be a science even of the "critical" kind. But if it is not the science of Being as such, of first principles; if it is not the critique of pure reason, meaning the structures of reason, or a transcendental epistemology; then it seems to me that there is very little left to refute in the thought of Hegel: maybe only his broadly "Kantian" claim to shut reason up in a stable image. If Hegel were not claiming an entirely determined and rational destiny for reason (and it isn't clear how far he pushed this claim), there would be nothing objectionable in the Hegelian vision of philosophy. It's a vision in which the only thing left to philosophy is a way of apprehending the historicity per se of all that comes to pass in human reality. Including science.

THE FLASH OF THE *EREIGNIS*

What I have said so far does not imply that philosophy ought to be cut off completely from science. Rather, it interests me greatly to learn *what the impact is* of certain scientific achievements, what has changed in the history of our existence, our culture, our human community in consequence. For me, the philosophy of science is basically, whether it likes it or not, a species of sociology or philosophy of culture. Philosophical reflection on science cannot just be the logic of science; Feyerabend was right to ask what business it was of philosophy to tell science how to think. Philosophical reflection on science should be historical reflection on the aftermath of the transformation of our existence by this strain of cultural activity. Naturally, this stance is part of my overall attempt to think in terms of the ontology of actuality, to answer the question: what of Being in a world in which the empirical, experimental, mathematical sciences have developed along certain lines and yielded certain technological results?

In this respect, I disagree squarely with the traditional image of the philosophy/science relationship, especially as Gadamer portrays it in *Truth and Method*, and Heidegger too, though Heidegger is more astute; his essay on "The Age of the World Picture" reveals a more receptive attitude to science.[2] Gadamer tries various ways of mending the rent between method (science, that is) and truth, but nevertheless the discourse in *Truth and Method* always comes round to a defense of his basic claim, to wit, that truth does not rest with science alone (and you can even bracket the word "alone"), there is truth in history, in aesthetic experience, in historical experience: truth lies in the experience of common, non-specialized language, which governs scientific language as well. This is the overriding aspect for Gadamer. Fundamentally, his stance is always a defense of humanism, though it may perhaps wish it weren't, and perhaps isn't at bottom.

If I turn to his short book *Reason in the Age of Science*,[3] though, our positions are a lot closer. Gadamer says something there to which I could subscribe, when he proposes to set limits of an ethical kind to science. The problem is not the truth or falsity of scientific propositions, or truth or falsity in the way science regards existing things; the problem is that science has social, historical effects, and on those an ethical framework demands to be imposed (not counterposed).

Gadamer rightly maintains that this ethical dimension has to do with the *continuity* of the spirit, with the fact that we are in this together.

> *The closed work place of the earth ultimately is the destiny of everyone.... We are still a far cry from a common awareness that this is a matter of the destiny of everyone on this earth, and that the chances of anyone's survival are small...if humanity...does not learn to rediscover out of need a new solidarity.*[4]

But the crucial point is that Gadamer doesn't really take onboard the meaning of Heidegger's discourse on metaphysics; for him, Heidegger's objurgations against metaphysics apply principally to scientism, or rather scientistic objectivism. There is not, in Gadamer, a true history of Being.

Even when he does concur with Heidegger in the analysis of where philosophy is now, Gadamer in reality limits his discourse to the fact that modern philosophy, since the sixteenth-seventeenth centuries, let's say, or if one prefers, since Kant, reduces the ambit of truth to the ambit of the experimental ascertainability of science. All the rest is outside the ambit of truth. This fundamentally goes for Heidegger too, but the idea never even occurs to Gadamer that this might have come about for some reason. In this sense, Gadamer remains moored to a static vision of the relation of mind to world; he isn't much of a "Hegelian." How does it happen that at a certain point we start thinking that the sole truth is that of the positive, experimental, mathematical sciences? Gadamer would say it is simply an error, and maybe it is, but it is certainly an error of gigantic proportions, with stunning consequences, which remain unaccounted for.

That falls a bit short, it seems to me. So when it comes to thinking about science, I feel much closer to Heidegger than to Gadamer, though even Heidegger probably could have done more in this area than he did. Science is an essential aspect of the destiny of Being in the contemporary world. But not just the destiny of oblivion, the destiny of a possible return, too. That is why I lay so much emphasis on that unique place in *Identity and Difference* where Heidegger says that the *Ge-Stell*[5] might be regarded as a first flash of the event of Being:

> *Das Ereignis vereignet Mensch und Sein in ihr wesenhaftes Zusammen. Ein erstes, bedrängendes Aufblitzen des Ereignisses erblicken wir im Ge-Stell. Dieses macht das Wesen der modernen technischen Welt aus.*[6]

> *The appropriation appropriates man and Being to their essential togetherness. In the frame, we glimpse a first, oppressing flash of the appropriation. The frame constitutes the active nature of the modern world of technology.*[7]

I inquired of Gadamer whether he thought Heidegger meant those words to be taken with full seriousness, and he told me that he had been present when Heidegger delivered the text as a lecture, and that Heidegger was clearly aware that he was advancing a singular notion. I suppose Gadamer might have given that answer to gratify me, or perhaps had not quite understood what I was asking him. But I take it at face value, because it's hard to imagine Heidegger just blandly coming out with the statement that the *Ge-Stell* might be regarded as a first flash of the event. For one thing, he says it that one time and never develops the thought. Yet it shouldn't be seen as an offhand remark. Something deeper is undoubtedly going on.

I hold to the view that Heidegger's words should be read in relation to his essay "The Age of the World Picture," which really means "pictures" in the plural. The natural conflict among branches of knowledge in organized society renders the world picture impracticable, it essentially becomes an image producing multiple images. All that talk about *das Riesenhafte* and *das Riesige* (enormousness or hugeness; that which is outsized or gigantic) in the final pages of the essay[8] is substantially saying that it is no longer possible to grasp the idea of the world picture—that we have produced the world picture, but this picture has then spontaneously, naturally, pluralized itself. . . . Hence there is no longer a world, there are multiple pictures of the world, and that generates the conflict of interpretations. Now all this is a question concerning Being, but Gadamer never comes out and states as much, and I wonder if he even could have. He remains closely tied to Plato, closely tied to Greek metaphysics, which also, of course, validates the idea that there are various apertures of truth. In a book on Gadamer, Jean Grondin says (without, as far as I know, any protest from Gadamer), that the idea of the plurality of the apertures of truth serves essentially to ground tolerance, to ground dialogue, in the sense that people grow disposed to accept that truth may inhere in more than one point of view. It's practically straightforward relativism; there is nothing historical, no history of Being, nothing about destiny. Gadamer never delved too deeply into this aspect of Heidegger, never took it all that seriously. It's odd, because on the other hand Gadamer declares himself a Hegelian: but his is a use of Hegel that minimizes this aspect of the problem considerably.

In 1985, in the first *Annuario di filosofia*, we published a translation of a 1965 essay by Gadamer on the philosophical foundations of the twentieth century.[9] Gadamer clearly does not adopt Hegel's open historicity, tending instead to reduce the stages ("moments") of the spirit to the objective spirit. It is not that doubt is cast on the triad of moments: subjective spirit, objective spirit, absolute spirit; it is rather that the absolute spirit is blanked out. For Gadamer the absolute spirit forms part of the objective spirit. You could read that in terms of Marxist historicism, that is, in terms of increasing concreteness: we are always part of epochs, and so we work in this "inside" that is history. But if the objective spirit develops no further, it too winds up as Aristotelian Being, a capacious (static) dwelling within which there are many mansions, *to on leghetai pollakos*. Naturally, this is how I portray Gadamer, an image I have formed for myself, against which I measure myself, with respect to which I define myself. It's not meant to be incontrovertible.

THE STORY OF A COMMA

Not long ago I wrote a brief essay entitled "Story of a Comma" for a special issue of *Révue Internationale de Philosophie* celebrating Gadamer's 100th birthday.[10] It is called that because when I was translating *Wahrheit und Methode* into Italian I was faced with the problem of rendering the sentence "*Sein, das verstanden werden kann, ist Sprache.*"[11] Should the commas be included in the translation or not? I have always maintained that they should, even if their presence in the original German is dictated by grammatical conventions that do not apply in Italian (or English), where strictly speaking they should be omitted.[12] So I raised the matter with Gadamer, and he disagreed with me: there was a risk of being misunderstood. Some readers, for example, might wrongly infer that there was a Being that was *in*comprehensible and that was different from language.

If you think about it, though, the only way for Gadamer to escape from relativism might actually be to interpret the sentence along these lines: Being, in its most general sense, has the character of being comprehensible, inasmuch as it is language. *Not*: only that Being that can be understood is language. For in the latter case, we would still be stuck with the distinction between the sciences of the spirit and the natural sciences; and more than that, the supposition would be entailed that somewhere beyond all linguistic comprehension there might subsist a Being "in itself." But saying that would mean returning to the "realist" metaphysics that Heidegger criticized, and that Gadamer cannot accept either.

My proposal to keep the commas amounted, in any case, to an attempt to read Gadamer in the sense of a history of ontology. And it appears to me that Gadamer, coherently with his own premises, ought to have gone down that road. But the step remains untaken, and Gadamer remains stuck halfway between relativism and Hegelianism. Gadamer's Hegelianism basically consists of arresting Hegel at the objective spirit and in understanding everything in the sense of *belonging*. It is an important principle, because it indicates the nonreducibility of philosophy to an act of reason, the impossibility of recapitulating the whole process in a self-conscious rational form of knowledge. "Belonging" means simply that consciousness is always *within* reality, and so it never succeeds in "exhausting" reality cognitively and comprehending it entirely. But it is not clear what the history of this reality might be. If this discourse (the Hegelian format of which is manifest: belonging is another name for idealistic-transcendental reflexivity) doesn't go all the way and admit the absolute spirit, then it is hard to see what its ultimate sense is. Of course, it has a legitimate outlet in a kind of practical Aristotelianism, which isn't a futile hypothesis because it does allow a fair number of opportunities, but in any case it always remains a discourse that stops short before it gets to its conclusions: conclusions that have to entail, and cannot not entail, absolute knowledge.

Absolute knowledge—or, dare I say it, weak thought. In truth weak thought appears to me to be the sole alternative to Hegelianism. That isn't so far-fetched, because if there is no process towards a final self-ascertainment of reason, all that's left is the idea of a weak ontology. And that holds good even if one thinks, for example, that the self-ascertainment must always and only be provisional. At bottom, one can perfectly well be Hegelian while thinking that the absolute spirit is the maximum of self-consciousness we have attained to date, and that when we attempt to unify the cultures, or demonstrate the truth of certain propositions, all we are doing is trying to realize the absolute spirit, to furnish a relative image of it (and a claim of that kind does not strike me as entirely erroneous.) Now clearly, any effort aiming at universal self-ascertainment, whether the latter is thought of as contingent or truly ultimative, cannot be without direction: the process has to be provided with development in some direction that pertains to all of humanity. But then we're forced to ask ourselves why the absolute spirit, let's call it the maximum of actual self-consciousness available to us, has to be our kind of knowledge and not that of the Dalai Lama. If we engage in debate with the Dalai Lama, what do we assert? In that case we have two absolute spirits, each of them minding its own business, and they don't communicate with one another.

In other words: if you are not to give way to a species of pure relativism, and yet you strip Hegel of the idea of final absoluteness, of perfect self-consciousness, what do you put in its place? For me, you can only resort to the idea of ontological difference that becomes a principle of movement.

SCIENCE AND "BEING-NOT BEINGS"

In that essay on Gadamer, which expresses views I still hold, I also allude to a sentence from *Being and Time* I have already mentioned:

> *Sein—nicht Seiendes—"gibt es" nur, sofern Wahrheit ist. Und sie ist nur, sofern und solange Dasein ist.*[13]

> *"There is" Being—not beings—only insofar as truth is. And truth is only because and as long as Da-sein is.*[14]

Here the parenthesis formed by the dashes is just as important as the parenthesis formed by the commas in the passage from Gadamer. I place a lot of emphasis on "Being–not beings." It has to be understood within the framework of a teleology, not as a straightforward constatation. Heidegger is saying: there is Being, not beings, if there is truth. There is Being to the extent that there are not just, or not primarily, beings.

Now let's come back to science. Science is science of Being–not beings, just as morality and politics have been. Being–not beings in the case of politics signifies that we replace our initial emergency agreement to defend our common interests with a social contract, which is a way of transcending the immediacy of beings, getting to a different place, so that it's no longer *homo homini lupus*; instead there is the authority of someone chosen by common consent, or else there is collective authority. Ethics too, if you think about it, has always been thought of as something that transcends the immediacy of impulses such as the survival imperative, and self-interest, and power acquisition—something that transcends immediate subjective avidity. Lastly, and perhaps most "completely," science represents Being–not beings in the full proper sense, either because it has become science of mathematical structures, repeatable entities that as such are quite cut off from the presence *hic et nunc* of things; or because the very *stuff* of science grows rarefied, with physics talking about inexistent, conjectural, or infinitely small entities, things right on the borderline of spiritualization. Jean Guitton has actually tried to demonstrate the truth of God's existence through the spiritualization of the material in science.

From the viewpoint of a philosophical ontology, all this gives us further encouragement to adopt a "nonabsolutist" perspective. "Absolute" ontology, Hegelian ontology, or to put it another way, ontology that looks forward to a conclusion, is always vulnerable to the notion that its time has come and that it must now be imposed on others, or must be imposed because it constitutes finality attained. Even Soviet communism was a kind of end phase of disalienation, and therefore couldn't "admit" the possibility that further disalienation might take place. But if one strips Hegel of the "absolutist" outcome, then I would have no objection to reading the absolute this way: truth is that which, every time, has taken into account all the objections and has either found a way to resolve them on their own terms, or in any case incorporated them. It's called dialectic.

The fact that there are more South Asians immigrating into Europe undocumented than there are Europeans being smuggled into the Indian subcontinent might also be a sign of the validity of the Hegelian dialectic, an indicator of the fact that our form of existence is more desirable than theirs. We can accommodate sacred cows within limits, a privation like that we can tolerate, whereas over there they die of hunger. But Hegelism itself undercuts that as an argument for Hegelism. There is an interesting solution in a book by Gianfrancesco Zanetti with the fetching title *Felicità amicizia diritto*.[15] Zanetti tries to show that extensional liberalism is preferable to intensional liberalism. By intensional liberalism he means the pure affirmation of the right of each person as a totality, a completely autonomous totality, with no account taken of his or her relation to the community.

Extensional liberalism, as he interprets it, involves other people too, and the general state of things. There is an old enigma: if liberalism admits all the visions of the world, then fascists have the same rights as liberals. Zanetti addresses it by maintaining that we should have a system in which it is possible to declare your own position, or even cut yourself off from everyone else if that's what you want (he calls that the right to be unhappy), and that the defense of such a system has a higher quota of acceptability, as a stance, than any other stance available. Likewise, when I say that we cannot do without a philosophy of history, but that the only philosophy of history we can profess is the philosophy of the history of the end of the philosophies of history, and that this is a positive principle, I mean substantially the same thing. It is not just "anything goes." It is that if you accept that anything goes, and more than that, articulate the thesis that anything goes, yours is the position best grounded in reason.

As far as the history of Being goes, these consequences seem to me legible primarily as the history of the weakening of Being, and in that perspective science appears in turn as a form of derealization, of growing weakness, of transcendence.

THE EDIFICATION OF HUMANITY

Naturally, if philosophy does not bracket science and all its results and achievements and consequences for existence, but does not regard itself as a science either, philosophical practice has some explaining to do: just what is it then? My own response is that philosophy is a discourse more *edifying* than demonstrative, it is oriented more toward the edification of humanity than toward enhanced formal comprehension and advancement in knowledge. Edifying doesn't mean antitheoretical, it doesn't mean that there is not a progressive acquisition of knowledge during the edification of oneself and humanity. Rather, it means that that isn't the sole or overriding objective. The "edifying," according to Kierkegaard, is the terrible, the disquieting, and under certain conditions, the sublime (i.e., the negative, which for him means the perception of one's own finiteness); at the same time, it is that which ameliorates and constructs. So it is not without its theoretical or cognitive side, but it is also something more, and something different.

In the final pages of Husserl's *Philosophy as Rigorous Science* there is the well-known distinction between philosophy as a *Weltanschauung*, a vision of the world, and as science.[16] It is telling that this distinction winds up being essentially ethical. Philosophy as a vision of the world is a grand construct, "aesthetic" with a whole heap of quotation marks, a creative description of oneself and one's vision of the culture one inhabits. It may shape personalities of a desirable, or even exemplary, kind in certain respects; but at bottom it amounts to an egoistic choice. It's as though Husserl is really saying: philosophers of that sort are dandies, at most they may become theologians, poets, writers, essayists. It's undeniable that his depiction of *Weltanschauung*-philosophy in those pages has many positive aspects. But one asks oneself: how is his own philosophy supposed to escape this risk of aestheticism? Husserl explains that one should instead dedicate oneself to cumulative knowledge that accomplishes small steps, small acquisitions of objective knowledge that will withstand the test of time.

Apart from anything else, the first objection that comes to mind is: why should things that last longer be better than those with shorter duration? When you buy an automobile, the longer it lasts the better, but that principle doesn't automatically apply in this arena. Someone from Frankfurt might accuse him of articulating the harshest version of compulsory service: you must serve a history that you will never completely appropriate, instead of finding your part in what has come about so far. But leaving that aside, I think of philosophy in terms fairly close to what Husserl seems to deprecate: as essayistic edification. That's why, for example, I'm neither shocked nor offended when someone labels me a journalist. My response would be that the Husserlian vision of *Weltanschauung*-philosophy needs some revision: if I speak of philosophy as edifying knowledge (hence neither "specialized" nor "cumulative," properly speaking), that doesn't mean that I see it purely as *Weltanschauung*-philosophy, or as an exercise in style. On the contrary, edification is linked to intersubjectivity, and so to responsibility, which Husserl assigns exclusively to "cumulative" science, to the philosopher who takes "small steps" toward progress in knowledge.

CUMULATIVE KNOWLEDGES

Actually, I don't even exclude a certain cumulativity in philosophy, not in the sense that the results obtained hitherto are irrefragable and reducible to systematic textbook form, but in the sense that philosophy would not even exist without a textual tradition. So as a historicist I feel myself a "cumulativist," but not the scientific kind. There is one thing, though, that all this tells you, which is that philosophy is not a natural *genus*, a cultural mode of knowing. It is defined solely by a textual tradition, with a terminology and a set of problems as corollaries. Nor am I entirely sure that they are problems natural to mankind: even just the the notion of the universality of the validity of a thesis becomes thinkable only if certain conditions of cultural pluralism obtain. In a traditional society, nobody worries themselves about the problem of universal validity: there are valid laws and traditions, and there are individuals variously crooked or crazy or half-witted or whatever. The problem of universality only arises once people have had to deal with incommensurable paradigms, or outlooks on life that differ profoundly from one another; but the authentic meaning of universality arises there too.

My spiritual director, a well-reputed Thomist, said to me that the *Summa contra gentiles* was a missionary manual, meaning a treatise in philosophy and rational theology meant to be serviceable to those who were setting out to convert Muslims. Because there had to be some sort of baseline from which to start. I am intrigued by the fact that rational theology blooms in importance in a situation in which religious cultures are clashing, when some sort of common ground with the Other needs to be found. Thomas Aquinas and many other past philosophers believed that this common basis was universally human. I would hazard that this universal human basis is maybe not so universal after all, in the sense that it is historically always coming about, and we are continually remaking it.

Science has a codified tradition too, and Husserl's own notion of a form of knowledge that advances would be meaningless without the idea of a common tradition. And for that matter, philosophical theses have their objects too. The opportunity for experimentation in the positive sciences makes it easy to talk about "objects," whereas in the case of philosophy it is not so easy to tell whether there really is an object there or not. Yet the distinction I have in mind doesn't boil down to a distinction between objective and non-objective sciences. It is well known that even the object of science is always defined in large part within a paradigm and out of a paradigm. Obviously it makes a fundamental difference whether it is possible to obtain verification or falsification by experiment, and for philosophy it isn't and never was. So there is a sort of double bind: as soon as philosophy starts to state propositions that can be verified or falsified, physical or meteorological propositions, it turns into science.

Of course there is more than one way to look at experimental verification and falsification. Popper's falsifiability, for example, strikes me as more of an *ad hominem* argument than an objective one. The falsification of a thesis actually tells you nothing except that that is not the road you want to take, that it is no use trying to get from Pisa to Milan by way of Trento. Of course it is grounded in something more than just your own or others' convictions, but you haven't gained any positive knowledge except by labelling negative knowledge as positive. In other words: I know positively that such-and-such is not the case; but that signifies nothing. If something isn't green, it can be any color at all; "not man" could be any other thing whatsoever.

So any modes of experimentality that may be accessible to philosophy aren't the sort that can be assumed to yield "objective" knowledge. I take it that philosophy can appeal to experience, indeed I am convinced that philosophy contains truths of experience, but experience is always already so subjectively and culturally mediated that it is pointless to speak in terms of objective "increments." Dialectic, for example, is an experience shared by the philosophical culture of every age, but it is just the experience that if you pose things a certain way (the way Plato, for example, poses the question of one and many in *Parmenides*), certain consequences, which are always *grosso modo* the same, follow. My eyes see, I see with my eyes, which aren't your eyes. If I say "I have a toothache," I take it for granted that you know what I mean, but I could never demonstrate that you do. These are, so to speak, *natural truths*, not in the sense of nature but in the sense of obviousness, an obviousness produced, to a large extent, by culture.

So I don't know to what extent you can still call it philosophy when you employ experimental arguments. Philosophy of mind, the cognitive sciences, for example—are they a philosophical discourse or are they what some philosophers have arrived at largely because of contingent and historical circumstances (for example, the decline and rebirth of psychologism in the neo-Kantian and neopositivist tradition)? I don't know to what extent such outcomes really have much to do with a necessity internal to philosophy, not philosophy as I understand it anyway, nor, I believe, as it has traditionally been understood in our textual tradition. I don't picture Kant letting himself be swayed by the discourse of a cognitive scientist.

2 | PHILOSOPHY, HISTORY, LITERATURE

TRUTH, RHETORIC, HISTORY

I wrote an essay once on truth as rhetoric.[1] It might look a little different if I were writing it today, but let's see if we can clear the matter up once and for all. First and foremost: I am convinced that truth is not a problem of political science, or even a matter subject to scientific demonstration. Truth for me is *persuasion*, and when I say persuasion, I don't mean "take it from me, sonny boy," I mean something more like "let's all lend a hand here." In other words: philosophical arguments are arguments *ad homines*, not *ad hominem*. By truth I mean truth as persuasion, but persuasion in relation to, and together with, a collectivity, not the art of persuading people to part with their money or something like that. Essentially I am talking about proposals for interpreting our common situation along certain lines and starting from shared assumptions. I will try to persuade you by mentioning the kind of authors you have presumably read and experienced for yourself—not the kind whose business is proving that $2 + 2 = 4$, the kind who were also seeking *an interpretation of our common situation*. Not just any authors, authors who have earned a permanent place on your bookshelf and who are linked to your own specific experience. So the truth to which I bring the discussion back is this: how can you still be saying that without invalidating the experience you had when you were reading Nietzsche, Marx, and Freud? Doesn't the experience that you got from reading Nietzsche (or Kant, or Hegel) now block you from saying things you might once have said and defended?

The question arises: what kind of *evidence* does this furnish? I answer that differently from Richard Rorty, although he more or less shares my premises. I regard truth in philosophy as the result of a form of *ad homines* persuasion, but persuasion grounded in a certain faith in the history of Being, faith in our capacity to trace (interpretatively) lines of continuity in the history of Being. To me, this faith corresponds to what some might call a kind of philosophical evolutionism: the classics, the things that have held out, weren't perhaps necessarily classics right from the outset, things destined to hold out, but the fact that they did become classics involves me, what I am is largely the fruit of their endurance . . . In this sense Gadamer is right to speak of prejudices and the objective spirit having a positive and foundational quality of their own. It was similar reasons that ultimately brought me back to Christianity.

There is a providence of sorts in history. And I don't mean necessary a priori laws, or contentment on the part of the winners that history has worked out better for them than it has for the losers. It simply coincides with what might be called *the sense of creaturality*. I didn't bring myself into existence all on my own, I was begotten by others, and that fact transmits heritages to me. They are the only thing I dispose of in the world, my sole patrimony, and I have to come to terms with it. I may contest them, I may go looking for histories of those who were weak and forgotten, and recuperate them instead. But even here, there's a saying of Jesus in the Gospels that I find telling. Jesus says that every scribe is like the head of a household, pulling new things and used things out of the closet, and he says that in precisely a hermeneutic context, where it is a question of interpreting some passage in the Old Testament. Philosophy is like that: there is no objective guideline governing the tradition, you can always rethink history, pulling out new things and old.

ARE HISTORY AND ONTOLOGY COMPATIBLE?

The point of all this is that philosophy is edifying discourse, but edifying doesn't just mean convivial or entertaining. Edifying is to be understood both in the banal sense of the term ("I exhort you"), and in the strict sense in which to edify is to erect an edifice. I have already suggested that construction as edification bears a cumulative meaning: it means bringing something new to what others have already built, and upon which others may build in turn; it is never an immutable basis. This is the famous distinction that Heidegger establishes between *Tradition* and *Überlieferung*, between *Vergangen* and *Gewesen*, between past as past and past as already-been: philosophy doesn't relate to its past as to a definitively ascertained basis, but as to an ensemble of possibilities that always offer themselves anew to interpretation.

Science too works with stratified interpretations, with a research tradition, with results piled on results that are re-elaborated time and again, and in this sense there is a continuity between philosophy, literary hermeneutics, and science. In every case there is a tradition. Science has the element of repeatable experimental verification, verification by an experiment that can be repeated independently of time, and that makes it look like history plays no part. In reality questions of language and historically determined approaches to experimentation do play a role in the experiment. But there is no doubt that science claims a certain suprahistorical determinacy for its results.

Now one should always be alert when historicity is being emphasized: maybe what's really going on is some sort of defense of onticity vis-à-vis ontology. When I say "Sein–nicht Seiendes," do I mean that we should neglect things in existence and focus on Being instead? Wouldn't that mean leaping outside history, which is ultimately the history of things in existence, not of Being? Science does indeed bring to light structures that are repeatable precisely because they transcend the history of concrete entities, so the "suprahistorical" attitude of science starts to look like an ontological stance. But if I counter with the objection that even these stable structures are discoveries arising out of historical formations, then once again I am basically promoting a history that is a history of entities and man, not Being.

Too much attention to history does in effect carry one far from ontology. This is the classic objection that structuralists make against hermeneutics, and it is also the critique we hear from the analytic ontologists today: how does consideration of the modes in which Being has been and is being thought help one to address questions about what is and might be? On another level, and starting from hermeneutic and Heideggerian premises: if I emphasize historicity to excess, I end up focusing too much on entities and neglecting Being. (This, taken to extremes, is the reasoning that impels Emanuele Severino toward a refusal of historicity and time.) So however you look at it, there appears to be an incompatibility between history and ontology.

But at this point the Heideggerian notion of Being as *event* reveals its force: if Being is really event, then it is Being itself that "is" history, time, eventuation. And at this point the polarity is reversed. It is true that history is properly about entities; but paradoxically, excessive attention to entities causes them to be seen atemporally, with the atemporality proper to science that guarantees the abstract repeatability of experiments and all that follows. To think that historicity menaces, so to speak, the vision of Being amounts once more to thinking Being in the form of entities, and as a function of entities.

MYTHIZATION OF THE WORLD

If we translate all this into a question of philosophical method or style, we are brought face to face with the reasons for preferring a hermeneutic conception of philosophy. The most illuminating way to explain this mode of argumentation is Nietzsche's announcement of the death of God. Nietzsche doesn't mean to say that God is dead because we finally perceived with clarity that "objectively he doesn't exist," that reality is constituted in such a way as to exclude him. Nietzsche

could not, coherently with his own theory of interpretation—
there are no facts, only interpretations, and if this too is only
an interpretation, so what?[2]—enunciate a thesis of that kind.
So the announcement of the death of God is rather a way of
registering awareness of the course of events in which we are
all involved, and which we do not describe objectively but interpret riskily as leading to the recognition that God is no longer necessary. The announcement is the shared acknowledgment of God's inessentiality in a world in which science and
technology allow us to live without the terror felt by primitive
mankind.

But in the Nietzschean interpretation, God is no longer
necessary, he is revealed as a superfluous untruth, on account of the transformations in our individual and social existence that have been induced *precisely by belief in him*. The
God who always functioned as a principle of stabilization and
reassurance was also the God who always forbade lying: so
it's in order to obey him that his followers also give the lie to
the fiction that he himself is. Who could present this complex and vertiginous argument as a poetic declaration of the
(metaphysical) nonexistence of God? Suppose the faithful
do finally dispatch God by recognizing that he is a fiction: in
denying him they also deny the power of truth, and so strip
their own deed of any truth. That is why the real world that
has become myth doesn't simply give myths credit, or assign
them the task of substituting for truth. What it does is make
room for the play of interpretations—which in turn presents
itself philosophically as just another interpretation.

On this view, philosophy arises out of the perennial conflict or play of interpretations, but it cannot consist of a free-

floating gaze from everywhere and nowhere at this play or conflict. And it cannot consist in some form of artistic-literary praxis either, since its specific goal is persuasion *ad homines*. So any assimilation of philosophy to literature is excluded: in a certain sense, and counterintuitively, the experience of the mythization of the world strips legitimacy away from any sort of aestheticism in philosophy. There isn't any real artistic or aesthetic arbitrium in the kind of philosophy that inhabits the play of interpretations. Rather, there is adequation to a "logic," the logic proper to Nietzsche's hermeneutics, where recognition of the essential interpretativity of the experience of what is true is recognized in turn as an interpretation, and where the theory of the historicity (of the horizons) of truth is received as a truth itself historical.

FUGUES

The expression "anything goes" is sometimes used as a shorthand caricature of where it is you ultimately wind up if you dare to adopt the hermeneutic stance in philosophy. But if you think about it, "anything goes" is just part of going, and doesn't affirm any kind of relativism: the expression "anything goes" is going too, along with everything else. And I regard this as an indication of Hegel's superiority over Kant. It amounts to stating that when I am conscious of what I am, I've already changed, because I am what I am plus the awareness of what I am, and that is the fundamental element in phenomenology, dialectic, everything there has been in philosophy since Kant.

It is also the premise of hermeneutics: there is not just a situation that discourse describes or depicts as though it were a mirror external to the situation itself. There is a situation composed of the situation plus its description and interpretation, and so on. Likewise, the moment I realize that the expression "anything goes" is one of the things that are going, there is a shift of viewpoint, and perhaps there is a nonrelativizable dominance of "anything goes," because you could say that the idea of an ensemble comprising the things that are going and the very expression that incompletely describes it "goes better" than the others.

I do indeed appear to be in search of greater descriptive completeness, capable of including myself as well; but there is an aspect to bear in mind. This drive to be complete (to include awareness and reflection; to include the expression "anything goes" in the ensemble of the things that are going) actually translates into the discovery of an inevitable incompleteness (I myself plus the awareness of myself together constitute something different, which must once again always be aware). So it doesn't ever add up to an adequate description of the situation, because the very concept of adequacy in play here has changed: it is not the same concept as that held by those who think truth in terms of adequation. "Adequate" here does not mean "mirroring," but if anything, "satisfying" at a certain point in the discussion. It means "persuasive," but with a fundamental reserve or liberty. Fallibilism, for example, the statement that "everything may be falsifiable," is not a description of objective states, it simply conveys the impression that what I was saying might be mistaken, that someone might turn up tomorrow to contradict what I've said. In this light, the best thing is complete nihilism, the position that "everything is interpretation, including this," which we may regard as equivalent to the version of relativism that says "everything is relative, and the expression 'everything is relative' is relative too." It is better because it disquiets me more, it means there is one less answer, and one more question out there to be answered.

SCIENCES OF NATURE AND SCIENCES OF THE SPIRIT?

In other words, self-awareness is never an adequate description, because it is always comprised in the game. Only the hermeneutic notion of interpretation manages somehow to take this into account, whereas it seems to me that other philosophical stances are always struggling to relay everything in descriptive and objective terms, and in so doing, letting things elude them, or refusing to see them. Indeed, depending on one's viewpoint, and better still, one could say that what tracks this movement most "adequately" (again, with a heap of quotation marks) is the *interpretation* of a certain notion of descriptive objectivity, not the rejection of descriptive objectivity as such.

This also gives rise, I believe, to a different outlook on the sciences. When we speak of objectivity in science, what we really mean is post-Kantian science, which no longer sees cognizance in terms of the pure mirroring of things as they are. The use of the word "objectivity" after Kant no longer implies pure adequative descriptivity. Now as I see it, objectivity is hard to separate from the availability of criteria of verification, and this availability is what specifically concerns philosophical discourse. In other words, it's not governable by science, it's not an object of scientific discourse. It is what you might call a second-order question.

The meaning isn't properly that "science doesn't think," but that the use of the technologies that are made possible by scientific research "isn't a technological question," as Heidegger always says. The essence of technology is not a technological question—the word "essence" here meaning the way technology is "in force" or "applies" its validity, and its "spread" as a general human effect. Now this validity and this spread aren't questions that technology either may or could decide. Does this mean reviving the distinction between the sciences of nature and the sciences of the spirit, with philosophy naturally sharing the point of view of the sciences of the spirit?[3] I think not, insofar as the difference between the sciences of nature and the sciences of the spirit, as it was formulated in neo-Kantian terms, was still conceived as a difference between the world of nature and the world of liberty: as if the world of nature possessed a necessity of its own, absolutely undeniable, hence absolute *tout court*. So the fundamental prejudice went like this: in the determinism of natural events, what science establishes (stabilizes) ceases to move. Ethics, on the contrary, naturally does move, it comes and goes, in other words it's free, and in the realm of freedom there is the noumenon that is ungraspable other than regulatively, as an ideal of reason.

I don't see that I can take my stance within that frame. From where I stand, that which occurs in the domain of the hard, experimental sciences is also the history of Being. And the history of Being has to do with the passing on of linguistic messages, cultural messages. Therefore the hardness of the sciences is not threatened in the least by my perspective, but nor is it taken to undergird an immutable natural order. I accept that it is grounded in a much *slower* pace of transformation of the criteria of objectivity: in the case of science, the criteria alter gradually, over long scientific eras, whereas in everyday life the criteria that guide me today might change radically overnight, through some further acquisition of understanding.

Philosophy is the self-consciousness (and self-conscience) of common language, more precisely the self-consciousness of the metalanguage within which all the specific languages are situated, define their stability, and eventually undergo transformation. So it is not even placeable within the traditional distinction between the sciences of nature and the sciences of the spirit, it is something markedly different that is implicated in both, because the "hard" sciences are interpretative sciences too, an interpretative way of knowing, not purely descriptive knowledge. The difference is that they interpret according to norms that, since they belong to specialized languages, are stabilized within the metalanguage and are not subjected to constant probing, the way reflection on values or on the meaning of life is. It may be a bit difficult to put this into words, but I think it is intuitively easy to grasp.

This doesn't signify in the least that physicists have it wrong, or that science doesn't possess a rock-solid objectivity. It only means that this objectivity is placed in, situated within, belongs to the history of Being as well. This morning my water heater wasn't working, and I had to check the water pressure, so this gets thrown at me: you too stand within the objectivity of the criteria established by science, because if science hadn't conceived of water heaters, and instruments for checking the water pressure, you wouldn't have home heating. True enough, all this is objective, but it is an objectivity constructed within a configuration in which there exist tubes and boilers, and in which objects of this kind are made into instruments for warming residences. In other words, every "natural" objectivity is also "cultural," in the sense that it is not objectivity given once and for all, that is either there or not, exists or doesn't, but is the result of a configuration given and constructed, and only within that configuration do certain events come about or not come about, and the yes/no alternative have force.

3 | LOGIC IN PHILOSOPHY

LOGIC AND THE LOGICS

For Nietzsche, nihilism potentially reaches an end stage, at which it is "accomplished," meaning completed or fulfilled. For me, nihilism is accomplished when the contradiction internal to the hermeneutic experience of truth is fully acknowledged. And that acknowledgment is a "logical" stance, if logic broadly means the mode in which we think truth, and in which we engage in thought and discourse in whatever contingent circumstances, historical and linguistic, are given to us. On that basis, the connection between truth and rhetoric adduced in the previous chapter does not take anything away from logic. But if logic merely denotes the technique of producing valid inferences, then certainly the assertion that truth is a rhetorical matter, a matter of persuasion *ad homines*, does remove truth to some extent from logic's area of competence. (And as far as that goes, it is well known that inferential logic has never been able to grasp the concept of truth on its own.) But what I described in the previous chapter as the connection between truth and the history of Being does not in the least rob logic of meaningfulness as the science of the logos, as reflection on the modes of thought available to us in the single historical apertures of Being, which are the horizons of truth and falsehood of a culture.

To put it another way: I myself have never invented a criterion on the basis of which to verify or falsify propositions, but I *utilize* criteria of this kind, and the fact that they are there when I need them is something that actually escapes my control. I can reflect on them, try to remold them, but I am unable to dominate and comprehend their compulsory force. It is my very existence that, already and de facto, gives me forms and criteria the compulsoriness of which I do not know and cannot establish. My relation to Being is my having-been-thrown inside a horizon of truth and falsity, where I have to deal with criteria already given—but it doesn't say anywhere that they are the only ones possible, or that they could possibly be normative everywhere and at all times. So if I understand logic not as the neutral and universal mode for speaking of Being, but as reflection on criteria given time and again, then logic is nothing more than a part of the ontology of actuality, and it's business there is to be constitutively suspicious, to subject the criteria of truth to ongoing, relativizing clarification.

It interests me to learn more, for example, about non-binary, many-valued logics; non-Euclidean geometries interest me too. The evolutions and vicissitudes of these formal sciences, these purely formal ways of knowing, could hardly fail to be of interest for the ontological perspective, for a hermeneutics focused on the history of Being. But more than anything else, *difference* interests me, the fact that there is difference among logics, among geometries, and that the domain of the formal, exact sciences is itself caught up in the history of Being. Conversely, I believe that these vicissitudes act in their own way on the history of Being. If scientific transformations in general affect our mode of being, and of thinking Being, those in logic and the purely formal sciences must do so even more.

If I were more at ease with formalism, and all the expressive possibilities offered by the formal sciences, I would probably find elements that would help me construct an even more serious ontology of actuality. I've often wished to encounter a logician seriously logical and sufficiently Heideggerian to make an attempt at collaboration feasible. Giancarlo Rota, who died recently, filled the bill to some extent.[1] But I can't set off down that road on my own. A philosopher can't treat the specialized sciences as if they were a tourist destination (taking a trip there out of curiosity, to see what others are up to), and if you try to be more than a tourist, you risk losing your bearings. I know people who began to get involved with Lacanian psychoanalysis, because there was a specifically philosophical side to it, and got lost in Lacanism. Likewise, if I tried to delve too deeply into logic, I'd risk becoming a lost soul, bewildered and bemused by a practice that ultimately has nothing more to say to philosophy.

If philosophy does have a stake in the differences among the logics, then it would be more worthwhile to know something about their history, and how different logics evolved. But that ought to be part of the professional baggage of an ontologist, just like knowing something about information technology, for example—and frankly information technology seems more accessible to me because I use it more often.

In some cases a degree of formalization may be useful for solving knotty problems in natural language that are otherwise baffling. For example, the argument that since "nothing is greater than God," then God must be so tiny that even nothing is greater than he is,[2] looks absolutely irresistible, and it is useful to find out why: why it looks compelling and why it fundamentally isn't. Apart from that, when I read texts by philosophers using logic, and when I can understand them, I generally feel like I am reading some sort of game or science fiction novel, a diverting pastime. I have friends who sometimes challenge me with mathematical quizzes that I find frivolous, and indeed as a philosopher I sometimes feel that that mode of knowledge is even a bit threatening.

Actually, the effect formalized discourse has on me is that I skip all the formalization and go straight to the conclusion to find out what the message is. And if I can't understand the demonstration in nonformal terms, the argument doesn't really convince me; in other words, I regard formalization as helpful in the way stenography, or a chalk drawing, or an illustration are helpful. But it remains ancillary with respect to common discourse. I am a believer in something Gadamer says: philosophy is a discourse of the language we use every day, of natural language.

LOGIC AND THE HISTORY OF BEING

So in sum: at the logicians' stall, there are formal systems on offer that they insist I have to use, even to speak of Being. I for my part believe that their systems form part of an epoch of Being worth learning about, but only so that I can better relate to Being through natural language. If formalized systems are to achieve rigorous construction, they have to see themselves as definitional and definitive, and avoid reflecting on their own history too much. So there is a kinship, but also a contradiction, between logic and the history of Being, and here it seems to me that logic runs the risk of all the "human" sciences that aim to become rigorous sciences: they tend to Platonize, to turn into sciences of eternal, stable, immutable structures. Paradoxically, the task of the philosopher today is a reversal of the Platonic program: the philosopher no longer recalls human beings to eternal Being, she recalls them to historicity. Even psychoanalysis, for example, has a tendency to describe the person in objective terms, whereas the philosopher is the one saying: hold on a minute, you yourself only came on the scene in 1900, when *The Interpretation of Dreams* was published.

Speaking of psychoanalysis: it is certainly a science of modern mankind because it originates together with modern mankind; but I always wonder whether it isn't also a science of modern mankind in the objective sense—that is, only modern mankind is an object of psychoanalysis. The same applies in part to sociology. Sociology works when it comes to describing societies already sufficiently complex, almost like class consciousness in Marx: it could hardly coalesce among individual craft workers scattered over the countryside, but in large industrial installations, it could. Sociology is the science of a society that is born at the same time sociology is born. Psychoanalysis is probably a science that comes about when social relations grow more complex. Norbert Elias's analysis holds up: a causal factor of overwhelming importance

LOGIC IN PHILOSOPHY

was the construction of the modern state, in which individuals no longer seek justice, or do justice, for themselves. That's where both sociology and psychoanalysis come from.

Can logic fairly be compared to those disciplines? Should philosophy be reminding logic of its own historicity or not? Supposing the answer to both questions is yes, then the conflict or incomprehension between logicians and philosophers can always be read as the Heideggerian problem of metaphysics: logicians want to state laws of thought that also apply to philosophers, and so philosophers are supposed to bend their necks to this yoke, but always on the unstated premise that the discussion is bounded by some kind of *static* rationality. This is the problem Husserl addresses in all his writings on the logic-philosophy question (with a nod once again to *Philosophy as Rigorous Science*): Are the laws of logic binding objectively, for a rationality divorced from experience? Isn't there rather a logical experience, a logic as experience, that is itself the foundation of logic?

Philosophy has one abiding query for logic, which is: supposing we do wish to describe certain objective forms of language and thought, there is good reason to think that such forms are not and never could be static and immutable. How can logic, purporting to be pure apprehension of the laws of thought in any setting, at any time, also purport to be a normative science? If there are eternal logical laws, I have to submit to them, and if I do submit to them, everything that determines who I am just evaporates, especially the difference between me and someone living 2000 years ago, or the difference between my actions yesterday and my actions tomorrow, my individual historicity and historicity in general . . .

It's on this level that the question of normativity arises: who decides on the use of one logic rather than another? It's like linguistic games. Games are many and various, but there is a linguistic game into which I am thrown right from the start—right from the moment I first realize that there is an array of linguistic games. So if I am thrown from the outset into this game, it's the game that comprises the fact that there are various games. Accepting that means setting discourse free from the requirement of adequation to a predefined rule capable of deciding the truth or falsity of whatever human beings say and do.

PHILOSOPHY OF LOGIC AND LOGIC OF PHILOSOPHY

At this point, assuming that logic as a unique (suprahistorical) description of (suprahistorical) forms of thought is inadmissible in philosophy, two questions follow. The first is: does the idea that there is a course of Being, a history of Being, not in fact entail the more or less self-aware use of a certain logic, or the preference for a certain logic? And the second: is there a specific "logic of philosophy" different from scientific logic? (Obviously logic is part of philosophy, but like every other philosophical discipline, it has the potential to regulate the ensemble.)

These two queries actually boil down to just one, as we see clearly as soon as we try to answer the second. It is true that philosophy perforce utilizes some mode of reasoning. This mode of reasoning could be called "the preference" for a certain logic. But it is also true that the logic that philosophy utilizes is the elementary logic available and prevalent in a given epoch. I insist on the privileged relation between philosophy and common discourse, which always overrides the link between philosophy and any specific kind of knowledge. On that basis, philosophy is obviously a historical way of knowing in many senses, and that includes the straightforward sense that it belongs within a certain historical horizon, of which it is aware and which it doesn't believe it can hoist itself up out of. The historical horizon also entails the *normality* (and in part *normativity*) of common discourse, on which philosophy labors not so much to adequate it to an ideal structure as to throw into relief whatever contradictions it may harbor, or to render it more coherent.

I've sometimes said, a bit provocatively, that philosophy is merely the prevailing ideology rendered a little less vague and confused, or put in order, or enhanced with some critical awareness. The underlying notion is that the prevailing mentality contains its own antibodies. For example, we know that we ought not to kill, and today we are mostly convinced that we ought not to make war either, and so on. This even applies to those who defend apparently opposite ideologies. If you encounter a Nazi, he will likely try to justify even the extermination of the Jews—but by describing it as a necessary measure, for example to eliminate the germs of violence buried in society. What this means is that even the Nazi ideology contains a formal acknowledgement of a value to life, which is perversely sought through wreaking violence. Nobody goes around proclaiming that the Jews have to be exterminated just because they do, end of story, or because the whole human species should be wiped out, or something like that. Naturally this is not a guarantee of anything; it neither legitimates nor even suggests the idea that there was any rationality in the Nazi ideology. But it does illustrate the notion that, in the very history of the epoch, in the very constitution of the most deviant and perverse ideologies, there exist potential antibodies, and that there is no need to appeal, when seeking a way to correct wrongs, to certain extrahistorical principles that we would find if we could hoist ourselves up into the world of ideas.

This seems to me relevant when it comes to philosophical reflection as well. I strive to modify the situation as a critic, not in the name of a principle located somewhere completely outside the situation, but in the name of a guideline of sorts that is somehow given to me in the situation. I am not entirely confident that it really always is given; I wouldn't entrust the government of the country to a Nazi. But what this does mean is that I can and should—as a critic—engage in discussion even with someone like him. I can't just classify him as an outcast whom I can shoot on sight, as Rorty sometimes seems to be suggesting. Admissibility to the debate has limits, according to Rorty, that Gadamer (as a German, perhaps) wouldn't accept. I'm basically with Gadamer on that, I could even try to engage a Nazi in debate. Naturally the debate might go badly, and if it does I'll just have to sink or swim as best I can, but the fact is that the moment I perceive (if I do perceive) that he too is oriented (albeit perversely) toward achieving betterment for humanity, all I can do is try to push ahead with the discourse. I have confidence that I will be able to make him see that camps and crematoria won't produce betterment for humanity.

So philosophy has a logic (of the norms of thought) that is historically rooted. That doesn't seem to me to contradict the notion of preferring a certain logic. I prefer a logic that stands up robustly to awareness of the plurality of logics, and awareness of the fact that I am living in an epoch, in a world, that allows for the plurality of logics. The discourse that includes all this, and succeeds in finding a guideline that includes all this—*that's the preferable discourse*. But it's not a discourse preferable in the absolute, it's a discourse that is absolutely preferable here and now.

So if anything, we should be asking: What does it signify ontologically that today philosophical logic functions as it does, that it "must" function that way? Is it a psychological datum that we are taking note of, or an anthropological one, or a cultural one? Does it mean "we all reason like that"? In a sense it does, but the fact that I can then ask "why, though, do we all reason like that?" entails that the question is suspended halfway between a description of how we reason and a vision of how we might reason differently.

This, as I see it, profoundly separates the hermeneutic vision of logic from the vision any analytic philosopher would propose: an analytic would stop short of talking about the history of Being. Even Rorty would think that was going too far. So is talk of the history of Being just ornamental, just an add-on? Is it not enough to talk about history period, about the history of the sciences and the transformations in ways of knowing? Well, things aren't that simple. Nietzsche tells us that "the real world has become a myth," but if I forget that the real world has become a myth, I am always in danger of mistaking the myth in which I find myself for the real world. It's like what Heidegger says about the *parousia* in the letters of Saint Paul: the messiah may not return in hard fact, but the promise and the expectation that he will keeps you from believing in every charlatan you meet. The history of Being is like that: it is not the history of what necessarily had to happen, it is occurrences that teach you to mistrust dogma and anything else presented as necessity.

Today analytic philosophers have more and more to say about ontology I am told, and I don't imagine they had much choice once they realized there is no other way to justify any kind of normativity and regularity in thought. That is what I take ontology to mean too, but rather in the sense that it is the encounter with an other (thing, or person) that my thought responds to. When Heidegger speaks of the history of Being, he speaks of a message that summons me. If that is the case, why on earth should ontology exclude history?

For me the only way to speak of ontology is to speak of the history of Being, not limit oneself to speaking just of Being. How so? Above all, and in down to earth terms: if ontology were not the history of Being, logic would only be the history of human psychology, only an account of the various ways we have been fumbling around the elephant in the room labelled Being. That creates difficulties, like whether or not the history of our fumbling has made any progress: are you really going to try to tell me that Aristotle was a lot stupider than Bertrand Russell? In the second place, everything flows from the existential analytic in *Sein und Zeit*: Being is not given except through us, Being is not given otherwise than in a thrown project (Heidegger uses the noun *Entwurf* and the participle *geworfen*), which is the same point as before—in this sense Aristotle isn't stupider than Russell—but which is thought from the point of view of the analysis of so-called immediate experience, the point of view of the simple question: what are objects for me? And the answer is: objects are instruments within a project, this project is linked to a provenance, and so on. So there is ontology, there are things, there is a Being that "there is," but this *ontological* is only given within a history. If I speak of ontology, I can speak only of the history of Being; if I speak of Being without history I impose silence on myself regarding a determining part of that of which I am speaking, or else I am being spoken and governed unwittingly by a story bigger than I am . . .

When both the analytics and we Heideggerians speak of ontology, we are actually alluding, more or less knowingly, to something with which there comes a dialogue, something against which we measure ourselves, something that puts on the brakes when we feel the tug of "anything goes." And this something is that with which we have to reckon. Those who speak of ontology without speaking of the history of Being are still envisioning it in a way that leaves a quantity of unanswered questions.

Their tendency to strip the history out of ontology makes it hard, in general, for analytics to consider the link between Being and language. In the wake of the discovery that Being is given in the thrown project, questions remain: from where does its voice arrive, and in what does its cogency consist, if it is not just the simple cogency of the senses, of empirical data? The hermeneutic answer is that it has to do with summoning, a summons that comes to me not just from words but from a lived tradition that I assimilate, recognize, and live out within language. So it is not so far-fetched to maintain, with Heidegger, that language is the dwelling place of Being. With historicity stripped away, though, language is just one more item in the toolkit, to be used when needed like all the rest.

4 | TO SPEAK THE TRUTH

Yet in the end, underlying all the debates between hermeneutic and antihermeneutic philosophers, there is always the question of truth as adequacy, and as I've intimated, hermeneutics might even enjoy the advantage of a concept of adequacy that is different and more complex. But on the reasons for preferring this stance in philosophy, the first thing that always comes to my mind is a phrase from the Psalms, "redemisti nos Domine Deus veritatis."[1] Why do I think that in philosophy there should be a certain frosty reserve toward the notion of truth as objective description? Principally for the reason already stated: the idea of an objective description of the situation is unacceptable because the situation is always being augmented by the effects of reflection: there is the situation, there is the awareness of the situation, and there is the awareness of the awareness of the situation, and so on. But it is more than just a matter of remaining "faithful" to the dynamic of the situation: others could then object that once again a "type" of adequacy was being defended, and that it is not helpful or appropriate to think reflexively in every case, about every situation. There are other fundamental issues at stake.

Clearly it serves me to know how matters stand, but it serves me *in view of something that is not inscribed in how matters stand*. I might point out that the most passive form of religiosity is also the one most rigorously descriptive and adequative: it's the attitude of Spinoza. If contemplating the eternity of mathematical truth as the necessary structure of Being is my beatitude, in other words my liberty, then my liberty is just *amor fati*, the acceptance, pure and simple, of an order imposed on me.

Schopenhauer had the right response to that: why should it be necessary to love nature as it is, merely because it is nature? In nature the big fish eat the little fish, I defend myself tooth and claw, and so on. You call that freedom? When you pick apart every proposal for achieving liberation through knowledge of how matters really stand, knowledge of the rational order of the world, at the core of it you uncover an enormous metaphysical reverence for the necessity that transcends us: things are like that, they can't not be like that, and I may as well be content because I *have to be* content. Well, why on earth should I be content? In reality, "the truth will make you free" ought to be rephrased: not "that which is true frees me," but "that which frees me is true."

THE ENDLESS BANQUET

I read all this in Heidegger. The existential analytic, with its idea of project and its identification of the thing with the instrument, is in a way a philosophical reading of the expression "the truth will set you free," but in the sense of "what is true is what sets you free." Naturally, once that premise is accepted, it follows that that which sets me free is that which helps me, drives me, summons me to construct a project I can hope to realize. It is the project of emancipation through truth, and evidently emancipation doesn't mean taking careful note of how matters stand. So what then does it mean?

Here is where I can no longer keep the notion of truth and evangelical charity apart. The only emancipation I can conceive is an eternal life in charity, a life of heeding others and responding to others in dialogue. In the Bible, eternal life is basically thought of as more like a banquet than a geometrical contemplation of objective truths. What point would there be in spending eternity in the abstract contemplation of God? I don't know what sort of foundation or ground all this might provide, but an emancipatory project of this kind certainly seems more reasonable to me than an emancipatory project founded on knowing how matters stand. Ultimately the only justification for knowing how matters stand is what Habermas calls strategic knowledge: I have to know how matters stand in view of my project, otherwise how would I be better off knowing how matters stand? It is no accident that in Habermas the substantial preference is for communicative knowledge. He would never accept my putting it this way, but communicative action is really not all that different from lived charity. Objective truth assists me in understanding how to live better with others. I am no longer able to view truth in any other way than that, and I do not believe that my doing so entails a particularly hostile attitude toward the truths of science.

Certainly, some might object that we are then talking about different things, that what I call truth others call friendship, or good company. But there is a purpose to retaining the same word, and continuing to talk about truth even on this terrain: in the end, keeping the two things separate would mean accepting two regimes, and accepting the idea that objective, adequative, scientific truth may well be immoral and savage. It would mean admitting that only in the domain of the sciences of the spirit may we talk of charity, of truth as a value, and so on, whereas in the natural sciences it would be meaningless. But if it were really meaningless, why on earth would I cultivate the natural sciences? Because I want to contribute to a common dialogue on this topic: obviously that is the soundest reason.

DO VAMPIRES EXIST?

It isn't true that searchers for truth are searching for any old truth at all. Brecht had a facetious remark, I think it's in "Five Difficulties in Writing the Truth," which I used to cite during the strikes in the 1960s and 1970s. If someone gets up in front of a crowd of strikers to inform them that two plus two makes four, he'll get jeered. Plainly that's not the kind of truth that's needed. Do vampires exist? Maybe, but that's a truth that might not interest me, and if I don't bother with it, that doesn't mean I am out to demonstrate that vampires do not exist, or that it wouldn't be useful to find out whether they do or not.

Therefore, those who say "I am interested only in the truth" are actually making choices, and choosing this truth or that one. And this leads to a question that has always given me food for thought concerning the objectivity of experimental science: how much does the concept of relative relevance come into scientific work? When we do an experiment in the laboratory, we don't bother to shield it against electrical impulses from Alfa Centauri, because we take it for granted that they are not relevant. But who knows, one day we might find out that many scientific results have been vitiated by a specific influence we don't yet know about from Alfa Centauri. It is only an example, and some might say that this exploration of the *conditions* (the concomitant factors and their relevance) is also subject to the progressive conquests of science. But once again, this merely reminds us that history comes along and modifies even the most robust results, and modifies how we make use of them.

Naturally Rorty and I drift apart on issues like this. He recently defended once again the thesis "the truth does not exist," maintaining that its exact meaning is "the truth should not be considered as a possible object of research."[2] I view this claim by Rorty, like other stances he has taken, as the equivalent of someone going around trying to straighten out the hind legs of dogs—as the therapeutic obsession of a certain strain of analytic thought that feels compelled to tidy everything up. To me it seems a contradictory position for a pragmatist, an expression of the kind that demands pragmatic refutation, but more than that: I'd like to see how Rorty can address his fellow men without talking about truth. For my part, from the point of view of the history of Being, it's something I have to deal with, seeing that I philosophize within common language without pretending to be able to turn common language into a language of truth—and to top it off, in the name of a truth that is meant to respond to the absence of truth.

In other words, the proposition "truth does not exist" is patently meant to be a descriptive, objective truth about the nonexistence of truth and therefore it is patently contradictory to utter it—never mind that truth does not properly "exist" or "not exist," but is, if anything, assertible or not assertible. What does exist is a common language in which these effects of contradiction emerge, and to take that into account is what's important. Thus it is possible for me to affirm that truth dies like God dies. And just as the death (and the birth) of God in Christianity is an aspect of God, forms part of his nature, likewise this contradictory death of truth belongs to the nature of truth.

The discourse becomes completely different. There is history, the meaning of which I must understand: I must account for why it is that today the term "truth" is used differently, and why it is in a certain sense *true* that "we no longer possess the truth." The history of Being is made up of incidents, things that befall, but they are not "accidents" that can be dismissed with a wave of the hand: they are events. Truth, with its history, is one of these events, and it is difficult to imagine getting rid of it.

5 | THE VOCATION TO PHILOSOPHY AND THE RESPONSIBILITY OF PHILOSOPHY

WRITING FOR THE NEWSPAPERS

It is no secret that I also write for the newspapers, and "professional" philosophers view that as something of a blot on philosophy. You start doing it because it's a chance to earn, then you keep on for ideological reasons, or to justify yourself, or because you discover that it is not such a base occupation after all. Actually, in my considered view, there is no difference between what I do when I am teaching in the university, and what I do when I write a column for a newspaper.

These days, the media presence of cultural luminaries is normally justified by the high status their scientific or scholarly achievement has won them. It is obvious that when Rita Levi-Montalcini offers an ethical or political opinion it isn't scientific discourse, but since she is a Nobel Laureate, people ask her things like which party to vote for. Nothing personal against Levi-Montalcini, but in general this seems to me foolishness: there are pure mathematicians who are pure asses, and who utter inane opinions about life. But I believe things are different when it comes to philosophers. At any rate, I for my part feel specifically authorized to do the job of writing what are (sometime scornfully) called "opinion" pieces as something proper to my profession and not a side benefit of being an established philosopher, deriving authority from work done in my own field. I think it is very important to emphasize this point, because it bears directly on my vision of philosophy, and on what it is philosophers are supposed to be doing.

As regards myself, I've always made it my goal to serve salvation, but not primarily my own. Often I've said to myself: I have to perform well as a philosophy professor, because it's my job. But ultimately "because it's my job" just means: because I am of service to someone. Now, from the time I began to study philosophy, I already felt myself an educator, and wanted to teach; hence my activism in Azione Cattolica, in the youth movements, and the jobs I held (and the volunteering I did) teaching young people.[1]

In reality I've always been a guest speaker, when I was in high school I used to go around giving talks on Maritain's *Integral Humanism*. That's how my philosophical vocation began. But whatever slice of my inner self there may be in my philosophical practice, whatever modicum of personal participation and involvement, lies on the border between philosophy and religion. That, I believe, gives my philosophical style and my writing their dominant tone.

WRITING IN THE FIRST PERSON

Only with *Belief in Belief*,[2] in 1996, did I began to write in a style that was not only unsuited to the genre of the treatise (sometimes I find I am unable to write treatise-style even when the situation calls for it), but also foregrounded the first person and reflected upon my own writerly situation. If there is a stylistic or literary "turn" in my philosophical writing, it flows from a kind of religious intimacy, but which I still manage to bind to philosophy. It's not out of the question that this may lead me to write differently in the future, and maybe to work differently in philosophy. About that I am noncommittal as yet, because basically, deep inside, I am diffident of my individuality, and of that which is personal. Weak thought for me connotes a certain intrinsic irony about subjective emphasis, stylization of any kind, and overly private and sentimental writing. When Derrida starts out with observations like "We are not far from Rome, but are no longer in Rome. Here we are literally isolated for two days, insulated on the heights of Capri,"[3] he fails to enchant me. Unlike Rorty, I am not a fan of the personal note in Derrida's philosophical style.[4] On the contrary I accuse him of literariness in the negative sense of the term. I should add that in general his texts show this defect only at the beginning; what he has to say subsequently is usually more to my taste. In a sense, the exordium on a personal note is like a sort of Wittgensteinian ladder to him, so I shouldn't be too harsh.

One always feels blocked at the start, of course, and hermeneutics helps one get over it by making an explicit theme of precomprehension, the act of setting down clearly what one already knows about the theme one wishes to address, and setting out clearly one's motives for wanting to do so. Sure, the easy way past the block would be to dabble in psychology and the sociology of knowledge, but I don't believe that extrinsic factors like that really cut it: hermeneutics is calling us to a different way of expressing the significance of the beginning.

The fact is that what we are really dealing with in our work, and not by accident but fundamentally, is primarily and predominantly the problem of the beginning. Philosophy is, still today, thought about the beginnings, the first foundations, and bears the weight of the whole system of second-order modes of knowing. And the second-order modes of knowing also have a philosophical meaning or dimension, inasmuch as, like it or not, they always have a problem of (relating to) beginning. When you get right down to it, what I called the block at having to begin has nothing to do with psychology, it is something specifically philosophical: it's the block of the existential condition, it's the character both personal and impersonal of thought in the effectuality of existence. In other words, it's the same image with which Kierkegaard critiqued, and at the same time reformulated, the Hegelian problem of commencing. From this perspective, writing in the first person is often just an inflection of the problem of beginning, just a way to render explicit the arbitrary (personal?) and at the same time necessary (suprapersonal?) nature of what gets said and how it gets said.

THE DIVE INTO POLITICS

To write in the first person to me means putting oneself in question within a common project, rather than what Rorty calls "falling back on private fantasy,"[5] or reducing philosophy to a textual practice for what Aldo Gargani calls "the redefinition of oneself"—goals of little importance, as I see it. I come back to what I said above about writing for the newspapers: in philosophy I believe that some political good is always at stake, some question of political community. That is what justifies philosophy as teaching, philosophy in the newspapers, and philosophy in politics too. It's this last bend in the road I find myself facing today.

I reject the notion that this is a *compensatory* move, a way to evade a certain objective and historical crisis in philosophy, as Rorty seems to have viewed the relation between Derrida and literature. From certain vantage points, to shift from philosophy to some other human science or cultural practice amounts to a (col)lapse or a capitulation. I once heard Pareyson say ruefully, when one of his philosophy students changed his major to history, "he fell into history." Imagine what he might be saying about me if he were still alive: that I have taken a dive into politics, without a doubt. But I am unable to share his outlook.

In my case, the continuity seems to me evident. I began to study philosophy because I felt myself caught up in a project to transform humanity, a program of emancipation. There might be a connection to my proletarian roots: it's proletarians who can't imagine really changing their own lives if they don't change the world. . . . If your parents are rich lawyers, you can say without any moral effort: I want to be a lawyer too. But if you're the son of a mother who was left a widow by a policeman who emigrated to Turin from the deep south, your own social unease motivates you to project a radical transformation; it's virtually preordained.

In any case, I began to become aware of who I was when I was reading adventure stories at the age of twelve. The answers seemed obvious then: I immediately began to imagine myself involved in an undertaking of historical and emancipatory scope, I wanted to help establish the Italian republic in 1946 and I wanted to help the Christian Democrats win in 1948. I was ten in '46 and twelve in '48, yet I could tell that something important was at stake in Italy in those years. It was mainly, I believe, the intense involvement of persons of religious conscience in the political project that Christian Democracy represented at that time, before the postwar reconstruction got under way. Later of course the Christian Democrats turned into something else, but back then the link was perfectly clear.

In a sense I was born philosophically within that outlook—which from the religious point of view had its defects, like being moralistic rather than mystical, for example. I basically enrolled in philosophy because it seemed to me a way to take these ideas further, and to do so as a professional, an academic. I wrote my thesis on the concept of doing in Aristotle,[6] because I felt I was part of an effort to construct a new Christian humanism against the Pharisees. Umberto Eco had a similar project when he did his research on the aesthetic problem in Thomas Aquinas. What was the upshot in my case? My original goals evolved into an affinity for the critical thinkers of modernity, and that was obviously something that was going to happen. Why would someone turn to Nietzsche after having studied Aristotle? Because someone who had studied Aristotle in search of an alternative to liberal-individualist, eudemonistic modernity, was pretty much fated to stumble across the critics of modern individualism.

There may be a certain Platonism about this kind of philosophical vocation. Plato is the supreme philosopher-politician, and while it may be paradoxical, it is not accidental that Plato was also the philosopher of Platonism, meaning of pure theory, of mathematism in philosophy. Be that as it may, I see the philosophical vocation as profoundly grounded in the *polis*. Philosophy didn't just happen to be born in the open "political" setting of ancient Greece. If we go looking for philosophy beyond the confines of the West, we have to stretch things a bit to find it. The Vedanta, the Veda, the Upanishads—are they philosophy? I am convinced that philosophy is a historical science, not just in the sense I've been proposing, but also in the sense that it is born together with a history of culture and a certain historical culture, and I don't know if it will die with this culture. What you might call Husserlian caution is always in order: something comes about, and it may not necessarily be ephemeral. Once medical science arises, people quit going to witch doctors, and that is a duty not natural but historical, a matter of faithfulness to history. It's also the only one we have, seeing that our knowledge of nature amounts to very little.

POLITICS PHILOSOPHER-STYLE

So, if this link between philosophy and the *polis* is clear, it ought to be equally clear why I can be drawn to theory without feeling that writing for the newspapers is a compromising activity for a theoretically oriented philosopher—and the historians of philosophy among my academic colleagues generally find me liable on just that point, calling even my theoretical interest "journalistic." Theory itself may be more or less "direct," or rather it branches into sub-disciplines. You can be a theorist and study nothing but logic, or epistemology. But I believe that, in any case, if you forget what drew you into your field, if you forget the political interest that spurred you, the religious interest, the emancipatory interest in general, you end up reproducing "the crisis of the European sciences": once again theory can't (in the best of cases) be anything more than a simple literary exercise, or artistic-philosophical experimentation, or (more commonly), an exercise in individualism for its own sake, serving private interests and power.

Philosophy, project, historicity, theory, emancipation— for me they all mean the same thing. And that of course makes fitting in a problem, and influences how I view professional status, the philosophical profession. In that respect I believe I have my shortcomings, but it is also the type of philosophical practice in which I believe that inspires many of my "nonprofessional" or not wholly "academic" decisions and positions.

One aspect that might be worth bearing in mind is that a purely political vocation is a little bit different from a philosophical vocation oriented toward politics, like the one I am trying to outline. The vocation to do politics as a philosopher, to work for emancipation as a philosopher and not as a dedicated political professional, to me meant making a choice that was somehow more universal, less directly involved, yielding fewer immediate political or legislative results. It was more educational. Pedagogy, the idea of educating humanity, of putting the transformation of mankind ahead of the transformation of structures, had a lot to do with my choice to do politics as a philosopher. My democratic intention pointed me that way, rather than toward direct, immediate involvement in politics: if you are democratic, your job is above all to produce what used to be labeled theory, meaning ideas, cultural stances . . .

Naturally a lot of existential randomness gets mixed in with all this; at any rate encounters and opportunities seem to play a large part. But fundamentally the differences and affinities between the philosophical profession oriented toward politics in the way I have outlined and the political profession properly speaking are easy to sketch. Above all, the philosophical outlook is more obviously critical of the state of things. Real politics involves making choices day by day, year by year, legislature by legislature, and at certain points it must inevitably close off debate about the pros and cons, stop feeling around for possibilities and make a decision. It's more pragmatic and less theoretical. At the same time, I've always seen myself as an ally of politicians, not as someone doing something completely different: it's simply that there was a *décalage*, a gap or a distance with respect to the immediate situation. In a way, I have to admit, this distance guarantees certain privileges for a philosopher: life runs a little smoother if you don't continually have to answer the question of what you would do tomorrow if you were the prime minister. Anyhow, I have the impression of working toward the same goals but at a different level. In 1968, when the students were occupying the university, Pareyson used to say "I am much more revolutionary than they are." I knew just what he meant and felt the same way, because we were reading Heidegger and thinking about metaphysics and how it had to end, and these in their way were projects for radical transformation.

Pareyson also had a theory of the specification of spiritual activities that justified his outlook in robust terms. For him, the doing or making that specificates (*si specifica*) as pure doing or making, as pure formativity, is art.[7] He was like Dilthey in assuming that the life of the spirit is a unity that specificates in the individual vocations and yet maintains a certain continuity. Just as, in making art, you express all your spirituality, likewise in doing politics or philosophy you express all your spirituality, nor could it be otherwise. So the fundamental idea was to maintain the unity of the spiritual life while knowingly accepting one's own finiteness, and therefore choosing and accepting one's own specialization.

When Dilthey speaks of historiography or art as ways of escaping the limits of individual specialization, what he meant was: spiritual life is the totality, it's the ensemble of the possibilities with respect to the littleness of your situation that you somehow summon up there before you, while remaining in your specialization. As I see it Dilthey was still too much of an empiricist to grasp the importance of this thesis, because he resolved the vision of the possibilities only in the imagination, in other words the imagination for him was the faculty of grasping the ensemble of the possibilities of the life of the spirit. In Heidegger there is something more: Heidegger effectively disrupts the situation determined by the contemplation of Being as distinct from beings.

A lot of what I have said to this point has its warrant in the notion that there is a unity to the spiritual life. I grew up cultivating the evangelical saying "to save your soul, you have to lose it." To me it feels drastic to say "I'm not coming this evening because I don't concern myself with those matters, they don't pertain to my vocation." It's like answering "Don't you know who I am?" It's impossible for me to refuse with equanimity when someone asks me to commit my time. I only say "I can't" when I already have another commitment lined up and really can't be in two places at once. But I choke on words like "that's not my vocation, that's not my specialty," and so on. They seem excessively egotistical, too self-important, even faintly ridiculous.

This has to do directly with the problem of the philosophical vocation in the current context of the teaching of philosophy in Italy. There are some who seclude themselves in their research into things like the historiography of philosophy because they feel threatened by too many calls, too many appeals, too much of a public profile. I understand them perfectly: barriers certainly do protect one's tranquillity, being a specialist must do the nerves a power of good (though you wouldn't know it from the concrete cases I've seen). It is sometimes said that the characteristic of philosophers is that they have a certain rapport (which may even be critical) with totality. Georg Simmel depicted the philosopher as "he who possesses an organ that perceives and reacts to the totality of Being." The ordinary person is always concerned with one thing or another, but the philosopher has "a sense for the wholeness of things and life."[8] Given that premise, it would be hard to deny that under certain circumstances there is something radically defective about narrow specialism in philosophy, and that is basically what I was referring to when I spoke about "losing one's soul."

I don't, however, believe that Simmel's definition can be accepted without reservation: in general one isn't born a philosopher, it's something one becomes. Pareyson used to say that those who sign up for a major in philosophy mostly do so after giving up on law because the lineup at registration is too long, and it wasn't an entirely facetious remark in my view. A vocation is made up of so many external and contingent factors: maybe if I had been rich I would have enrolled in medicine or some other faculty where they take attendance at lectures. One of the reasons I enrolled in the faculty of Letters and Philosophy was certainly that I could skip lectures but still sit the exams, and I needed gainful employment. We tend to forget how much is fortuitous in every vocation: naturally, as Pareyson also used to say, all that fortuitousness becomes a vocation when you interpret it and shoulder it.

FILLING IN THE BLANKS

Fortuitous circumstances, though, are mostly just the start of a trajectory that is driven much more by necessity, in form and in detail, than it may appear to be at the outset. There is a *contingency* in every professional vocation that transforms in part, or may transform, into *necessity*. For example there is a certain determinism in the affinities that one goes on to discover, or forge. Heidegger's "vocation" came from theology, from an initial philosophical-theological-religious inclination that left an indelible imprint on the kind of philosophy he did. Husserl practiced an entirely different philosophy, and he began as a mathematician. This implies a further qualification, a specification of the route: chance becomes necessity, but it doesn't just become a generic vocation to do philosophy, it becomes a road, a cultural and spiritual path.

Reflecting on Husserl and his origins as a mathematician, I sometimes find myself wondering whether what he did was really "philosophy." For me the only philosophy, the only way of doing philosophy, is the one I have described, which arises out of religion and politics. Moreover: I believe that this way of thinking and practicing philosophy is what distinguishes it from any other scholarly or scientific profession. In that respect I disagree with what Husserl says in *The Crisis of the European Sciences*, to the effect that there are the scholars and scientists, and then there are the philosophers, the "functionaries of humanity." I believe, on the contrary, that whoever is not doing philosophy is a diminished human being, or a "lowly laborer." Any effort to gaze tolerantly on the other human conditions seems to me slightly hypocritical. I am convinced that when you get right down to it, nobody can seriously "specialize" unless they are permnanently alive to the totality of spiritual life: that is what's "philosophical" in every human life.

Naturally I don't regard my doctor friends, or chemist friends, or cyclist friends as poor wretches. But I do ask myself what those who don't do my job have on their minds when they are not doing their jobs. What does a poultry-retailer do when he's not retailing poultry? I sometimes think that the importance of eros in the lives of persons lies in the fact that it fills up exactly those blank spaces that aren't filled by work.

Now philosophy is what you are thinking about when you have nothing else in particular to think about. . . . In that sense, perhaps doing philosophy corresponds not so much to a talent or a vocation as to a defect, or rather the reinforcement and institutionalization of a defect. In philosophy, what is being thought "professionally" is the interludes of existential specification, when professional specialization is dormant and the totality of spiritual life assumes higher relief.

Evidently an inclination of this kind only occurs in a certain kind of society, under specific cultural conditions. If the academic study of philosophy did not exist, if it weren't notionally feasible as a profession, nobody would dream of emphatically qualifying the absence of specific thoughts as thought. So, once again, philosophy is merely historical finiteness in its pure state.

Sometimes I wonder if I'm a parasite, and it isn't just an ironic pose—I mean, the question comes to mind: how long will the government continue to pay the salaries of philosophy professors? Philosophy certainly isn't a "natural" profession. It's not just an oddity that philosophers in the past ground lenses for a living, and there's always a hint of dilettantism clinging to philosophy that imparts an instability to the trade. The fact is that while the problem of *The Crisis of the European Sciences*, in other words that of holding one's own specialty in relation to the totality of spiritual life, may be marginally present in every profession, in philosophy it is structural.

Yet when I ponder these problems of specialization and non-specialization, I realize with dismay that I am only talking about 0.0001 percent of humanity. There are people for whom the problem of specialization doesn't arise because their problem is paid work of any kind. There's a mass of unskilled labor in the world and *Bildung* is the last thing on their mind because they are living hand to mouth. Would my aunt, who was a worker in a factory making socks, even have understood this problem?

The life of most of humanity is spiritually fulfilled by religion and eros: an oscillation between the afterlife of the soul and the survival of the species. In villages where people are dying of hunger, what sense could a problem of this kind have? I myself am sometimes appalled at the narrowness of the horizons that bound my own reflections: I'm the one preaching "loss of soul," but I spend my time talking about myself and those who ply trades on the same spectrum as mine—civil servants in other fields, or professionals, or even workers at Fiat. But the bottom layer of the proletariat, primitive peoples, the urban poor squatting in the streets of Calcutta, what could the things I am talking about ever matter to them?

So, cards on the table: it's my belief that when I do philosophy, I produce a discourse that only matters to a certain slice of the world, and that's all. True, philosophy legitimately and dutifully proposes to be a universal discourse, but only inasmuch as it cannot be. Such is the pressure of the whole, of the totality of spiritual life. How do I relate myself to the question of the urban poor squatting in the streets of Calcutta, whether or not it's raining, whether or not there's anything to eat? What do I think of my universality vis-à-vis that? I think a bit like Husserl thinks when he talks about the witch doctors and the medical doctors, in other words they would need to have the capacity to compare their existence with mine. And it is my ineluctable belief that they would choose mine, or at any rate would choose a kind of awareness capable of entering into dialogue with me, and with other forms of awareness. I do not feel myself more evolved than primitive peoples, but I do think that even just the possibility of communication, of imagining a possible communication with different cultures, puts me in a position of privilege, and basically a certain primacy.

The idea of universality as a construct, of the universal as task or project or guiding idea—the idea fundamentally driving all of philosophical culture since Kant—must be bound rigorously to a political project. Indeed, it demands to be recognized as a political construct to all intents and purposes. This is not a eurocentric idea, even if it is a product of Europe. And it has an objective correlative. Right now we have the problem of technological universality, which has the capacity to spread without bearing with it the value horizons that have made it possible in the West, or is threatening to spread without bearing them, or may be quite incapable of bearing them. When the Japanese master electronic technology but not democracy, a properly *philosophical* problem is presented.

I believe that philosophy has plenty of work to do here. And the European Parliament is an ideal place for it to get done, because it is much more about trust in the possibility of modifying customs and cultures than it is about legislative platforms. The relative vacuity of what goes on in the European Parliament is sometimes disconcerting: a lot of money gets spent on just uttering declarations. If you think about it, though, it is a lot like philosophy: less immediately efficacious on the plane of day-to-day politics, but a source of hope that vaster projects bringing change in the long term may be realized. Philosophical responsibilities are like that, you have to shoulder them even when it doesn't feel particularly gratifying and costs a lot of effort.

NOTES

INTRODUCTION: THE STRONG REASONS FOR WEAK THOUGHT

1. That the metatheoretical ground of weak thought is quite strong is by now an established point. Cf. Aldo Magris, "I forti impegni del pensiero debole. Un seminario di Gianni Vattimo a Venezia," *aut-aut* 273-274 (1996). Magris emphasizes the fundamentally Hegelian premises of Vattimo's discourse, an aspect to which I shall return, and which Vattimo confirms at pp. 57-59. See also Dario Antiseri, *Le ragioni del pensiero debole: Domande a Gianni Vattimo* (Rome: Borla, 1993); Gianfranco Basti and Antonio Perrone, *Le radici forti del pensiero debole: Nichilismo e fondamenti della matematica* (a special issue of *Con-tratto*, 1992); Anne Staquet, *La pensée faible de Vattimo e Rovatti: Une pensée fable* (Paris: L'Harmattan, 1996).

2. This is the critique legible between the lines of the final pages of the essay by Luigi Pareyson, "La filosofia e il problema del male," *Annuario filosofico* 2 (1996).

3. See essentially the following texts: Vattimo, "Dialettica, differenza, pensiero debole," in *Il Pensiero Debole*, ed. Gianni Vattimo and Pier Aldo Rovatti (Milan: Feltrinelli, 1983); Vattimo, *Oltre l'interpretazione: Il significato dell' ermeneutica per la filosofia*

(Rome: Laterza, 1994). English translation: *Beyond Interpretation: The Meaning of Hermeneutics for Philosophy,* trans. David Webb (Stanford: Stanford University Press, 1997); Vattimo, "Le deboli certezze," in *Alfabeta* 67 (1984); Vattimo, "Perché 'debole','' in *Dove va la filosofia italiana?*, ed. J. Jacobelli (Rome: Laterza, 1996.

4. [*Oltrepassare* and *oltrepassamento*, words the author uses frequently in this essay, mean both "to surpass, the surpassing," and "to overtake, the overtaking." But as used here they also have the connotation of "leapfrogging," a recurrent pattern or play of overtaking and being overtaken, and while I avoid "leapfrogging" as a translation, readers should bear that in mind. WM]

5. Unlike Vattimo, I think that there does exist an "objectivity" of certain (good or bad) philosophical "discoveries," like dialectic. I believe that in this context, by which I mean the tendency of the third philosophical level to collapse back to the first, Hegel's dialectic constitutes an objective acquisition. This applies to philosophical arithmetic: if the terms of reference are changed, and we focus on existentiality, for example, then of course matters stand differently. At p. 67 Vattimo comes close to admitting that dialectic has a certain objectivity, albeit subordinated to historico-linguistic premises.

6. See pp. 15–22.

7. That of Stanley Fish, for example, who is still perhaps the most radical defender of the position that "all is interpretation" (or ones analogous to it). See his recent *The Trouble with Principle* (Cambridge: Harvard University Press, 1999).

8. Claudio Ciancio, in *Il paradosso della verità* (Turin: Rosenberg and Sellier, 1999), has clearly illustrated this triple level of discourse, showing how the viewpoint of hermeneutic ontology

(the background or framework of the thought of Pareyson and of Vattimo himself) is not and cannot be the simple disavowal of all objectivity, but if anything the collocation of objectivity at a different level, in a meta-discourse of a particular kind.

9. "Philosophy at the start of the millennium" was the title of the collection in which this book first appeared in 2000.

10. [Or the zizania, darnel, vetch, or tares, according to the Bible version one is using. The reference is to the parable of the weeds and the wheat in Matthew 13:24–30. WM]

11. Vattimo may be defined, with a few qualifications that will emerge in what follows, as a typical "ironic" philosopher as delineated by Richard Rorty in *Contingency, Irony, and Solidarity* (New York: Cambridge University Press, 1989).

12. Vattimo, *Beyond Interpretation*, 6.

13. Vattimo's 1964 Royaumont conference paper appears as chapter 4 of his *Dialogue with Nietzsche*, trans. William McCuaig (New York: Columbia University Press, 2006). Royaumont was followed by the renowned 1972 Nietzsche conference, lasting a week, at Cerisy-la-Salle.

14. The impact of neostructuralism in American philosophical culture is responsible both for the postmodernist wave and the success of Derridean deconstruction: two philosophical (and cultural) tendencies that have unquestionably contributed to a harshening of relations between analytical philosophy and continental philosophy, causing a shift at a certain point from tranquil indifference to polemical opposition.

15. One of the best critique of neostructuralism or poststructuralism is Pascal Engel's "The Decline and Fall of French Nietzscheo-Structuralism," in *European Philosophy and the American Academy*, ed. Barry Smith (LaSalle, Ill.: The Hegeler

Institute/The Monist Library of Philosophy, 1994). Engel develops the point partly by expressing regret for the missed opportunities in the trajectory of Deleuze's thought. Vattimo briefly sets out not-dissimilar views in his introduction to the 1998 reprint of the Italian translation of Derrida's *L'écriture et la différence* (1967), *La scrittura e la differenza*, trans. Gianni Pozzi, introduction by Gianni Vattimo (Turin: Einaudi, 1998).

16. Gilles Deleuze, *Nietzsche and Philosophy*, rev. ed., trans. Hugh Tomlinson (New York: Columbia University Press, 2006). Original title: *Nietzsche et la philosophie* (Paris: PUF, 2005; first published 1962).

17. Perhaps the only really coherent position in polemics of this type is that of personalities like Antonin Artaud, who ultimately lived out with temerity, and in person, contradictions of this kind.

18. The point is emphasized in Enrico Berti, *Le vie della ragione* (Bologna: Il Mulino, 1987), 176–178.

19. Gianni Vattimo, *The Adventure of Difference: Philosophy after Nietzsche and Heidegger*, trans. Cyprian Blamires with the assistance of Thomas Harrison (Baltimore: Johns Hopkins University Press, 1993). [I modify the Blamires translation, in some cases extensively, in the passages quoted. WM] Italian original: *Le avventure della differenza: Che cosa significa pensare dopo Nietzsche e Heidegger* (Milan: Garzanti, 1980).

20. On difference in ontology, theology, and logic, see Virgilio Melchiorre, ed., *La differenza e l'origine* (Milan: Vita e Pensiero, 1987).

21. Published in *Wegmarken* (Frankfurt: Vittorio Klostermann, 1976; rev. ed. 1996; vol. 9 of the Heidegger Gesamtausgabe). (For full details on the volumes of the Heidegger Gesamtausgabe, see http://www.klostermann.de/heidegger/gesamt.htm.) Eng-

lish translation: *Pathmarks*, ed. and trans. William McNeil (New York: Cambridge University Press, 1998). "On the Essence of Ground" is McNeil's translation of "Vom Wesen des Grundes." An alternative English translation, the one used by the translators of Vattimo's *The Adventure of Difference*, is "The Essence of Reasons."

22. Vattimo, *The Adventure of Difference*, 63.

23. Ibid., 63–64.

24. See especially Gilles Deleuze, *Difference and Repetition*, trans. Paul Patton (New York: Columbia University Press, 1994); *Différence et répétition* (Paris: PUF, 2008; first published 1968); *Critique et clinique* (Paris: Éditions de Minuit, 1993). In *Difference and Repetition* and *Critique et clinique*, Deleuze displays his unwillingness to accept the particular post-Kantian dimension within which Heidegger's ontological proposition is located. See Vattimo's critique of Deleuzian ontologism in his *Al di là del soggetto: Nietzsche, Heidegger, e la ermeneutica* (Milan: Feltrinelli, 1981), 31–32. On the problematic of difference in contemporary French philosophy, see C. Sini, "Identità e differenza nella filosofia francese contemporanea," and F. Borutti, "Il nichilismo ontologico" in Melchiorre, *La differenza e l'origine*. [Books in English by and about Gilles Deleuze published by Columbia University Press include Adrian Parr, ed., *The Deleuze Dictionary* (2006), with an entry on "difference." WM]

25. Emanuele Severino's most important texts on this theme are *Gli abitatori del tempo: Cristianesimo, marxismo, tecnica*, 3rd ed. (Rome: Armando, 1989; 1st ed., 1978); *La struttura originaria,* new expanded ed. (Milan: Adelphi, 2007; 1st ed.,1958); *Essenza del nichilismo,* new expanded ed. (Milan: Adelphi, 1995; 1st ed., 1972).

26. Vattimo, *The Adventure of Difference*, 64–65.

27. See above all Vattimo's introductory essay, "L'ontologia erme-neutica nella filosofia contemporanea," and his afterword, "Pos-tilla 1983," in Hans-Georg Gadamer, *Verità e metodo*, trans. Gi-anni Vattimo (Milan: Bompiani, 1983; originally published in 1972); and "Hermeneutical Reason/Dialectical Reason," and "Dialectic and Difference," both in *The Adventure of Difference*. On this topic, I note the evolution of Vattimo's views from a position of what I would call latent and not-so-latent sympathy for Hegelianism, to a marked distancing from Hegel (coinciding perhaps with Vattimo's closer contact with French philosophy), and finally an ever more pronounced turning back to Hegel. On the profoundly Hegelian intonation of weak thought in Vatti-mo's version, see Magris, "I forti impegni del pensiero debole."

28. Vattimo, *The Adventure of Difference*, 166.

29. Ibid., 175.

30. Ibid., 168.

31. Vattimo and Rovatti, *Il Pensiero Debole*, 8. From the editors' introduction.

32. The divergences and affinities between Vattimo and Rovatti in the acceptation they give to the term "weak" are well ex-pounded in Staquet, *La pensée faible de Vattimo e Rovatti*.

33. Pier Aldo Rovatti in *Il Pensiero Debole*, 50.

34. Elsewhere Rovatti gives a more strictly ethico-aesthetic version of weak thought; see Pier Aldo Rovatti and Alessandro Dal Lago, *Elogio del pudore: Per un pensiero debole* (Milan: Feltrinelli, 1989).

35. Umberto Eco in *Il Pensiero Debole*, 79.

36. Gianni Carchia in *Il Pensiero Debole*, 89.

37. On Gödel's idealism and the nexus of dialectic and recursivity, see M. Kosok, "La formalizzazione della logica dialettica hegeli-

ana," in *La formalizzazione della dialettica: Hegel, Marx, e la logica contemporanea*, ed. D. Marconi (Turin: Rosenberg and Sellier, 1979); Palle Yourgrau, *The Disappearance of Time: Kurt Gödel and the Idealistic Tradition of Philosophy* (New York: Cambridge University Press, 1991); H. Wang, *A Logical Journey: From Gödel to Philosophy* (Cambridge: MIT Press, 1996).

38. Vattimo, "Dialettica, differenza, pensiero debole," in *Il Pensiero Debole*, 12.

39. Ibid., 17.

40. Ibid., 16.

41. ". . . la questione della riappropriazione e del proprio (coerenza-consistenza)."

42. On the evolution of the rational antinomy as an alternative to Hegel, see Claudio Ciancio, *Il paradosso della verità* (Turin: Rosenberg and Sellier, 1999).

43. Gianni Vattimo, *The End of Modernity: Nihilism and Hermeneutics in Postmodern Culture*, trans. with an introduction by Jon R. Snyder (Baltimore: Johns Hopkins University Press, 1988). [I modify the Snyder translation, in some cases extensively, in the passages quoted. WM]. Italian original: *La fine della modernità: Nichilismo ed ermeneutica nella cultura post-moderna* (Milan: Garzanti, 1985).

44. Gianni Vattimo, *The End of Modernity*, 23.

45. Ibid., 25.

46. Ibid.

47. Jean-François Lyotard, *La Condition postmoderne: Rapport sur le savoir* (Paris: Éditions de Minuit, 1979); English translation: *The Postmodern Condition. A Report on Knowledge,* trans. Geoff Bennington and Brian Massumi, foreword by Fredric Jameson (Minneapolis: University of Minnesota Press, 1984).

48. On postmodernism in philosophy and Vattimo's stance in particular, see especially Giovanni Fornero, "Postmoderno e filosofia," in Nicola Abbagnano and Giovanni Fornero, *Storia della Filosofia*, ed. Nicola Abbagnano, vol. 4.2 (Turin: UTET, 1996).

49. [See Friedrich Nietzsche, *The Will to Power*, trans. R. J. Hollingdale and Walter Kaufmann, ed. Walter Kaufmann (New York: Vintage Books, 1968), 8: "Since Copernicus man has been rolling from the center toward X." ("X" stands for "the unknown.") Kaufmann's note directs readers to *Genealogy of Morality* 3.25 for an elaboration of the thought. WM]

50. Vattimo, *The End of Modernity*, 164.

51. Ibid., 166.

52. Ibid.

53. This point is emphasized especially in Antiseri, *Le ragioni del pensiero debole*; see also Fornero, "Postmoderno e filosofia."

54. Vattimo, "Dialettica, differenza, pensiero debole," in *Il Pensiero Debole*, 21.

55. Ibid., 22.

56. Vattimo, *Beyond Interpretation: The Meaning of Hermeneutics for Philosophy*, trans. David Webb (Stanford: Stanford University Press, 1997). Italian Original: *Oltre l'interpretazione: Il significato dell'ermeneutica per la filosofia* (Rome: Laterza, 1994).

57. Vattimo, "Diritto all'argomentazione" in *Filosofia '92*, ed. Gianni Vattimo (Rome: Laterza, 1993).

58. Ibid., 63–64.

59. Ibid., 62.

60. Ibid., 60.

61. Ibid., 66.

62. Ibid., 68.

63. Ibid., 67.

64. The book was given a flat title in English: *Belief*, trans. Luca D'Isanto and David Webb (Stanford: Stanford University Press, 2000). Italian original: *Credere di credere* (Milan: Garzanti, 1996).

65. Read at the conference *2000 ans après quoi?* in Paris, December 1999.

66. I have attempted to clarify the extent to which this aspect should be regarded as a specific novelty with respect to the evolution of philosophical praxis after Kant in my "Theoria, teoria, transtheoria," in *Lettera Matematica Pristem* 30 (1999). My observations here about nihilism should be enough, I think, to refute the analogy which might come to mind between this form of hermeneutic Hegelianism and the pragmatic Hegelianism of Richard Rorty. See as well Robert Brandom, *Making It Explicit: Reasoning, Representing, and Discursive Commitment* (Cambridge: Harvard University Press, 1997). Vattimo gauges the distance between himself and Rorty at p. 99.

67. For more detailed analyses, see Santiago Zabala, *The Remains of Being: Hermeneutic Ontology after Metaphysics* (New York: Columbia University Press, 2009); Giovanni Giorgio, *Il pensiero di Gianni Vattimo: L'emancipazione dalla metafisica tra dialettica ed ermeneutica* (Milan: Franco Angeli, 2006); T. G. Guarino, *Vattimo and Theology* (New York: Continuum, 2009); and see as well the essays in Silvia Benso and Brian Schroeder, eds., *Between Nihilism and Politics: The Hermeneutic of Gianni Vattimo* (Albany: SUNY Press, 2010).

68. Gilles Deleuze, *Nietzsche and Philosophy*; and Jean-François Lyotard, *Des dispositifs pulsionnels* (Paris: Bourgois, 1980).

69. See note 47 above.

70. On the differences and similarities see Zabala, *The Remains of Being*.

71. Vattimo, "Introduction" to Franca D'Agostini, *Analitici e continentali* (Milan: Raffaello Cortina 1997).

72. In Jeff Malpas and Santiago Zabala, eds., *Consequences of Hermeneutics: Fifty Years after Truth and Method* (Evanston: Northwestern University Press, 2010).

73. The ontological bases of weak thought are specifically investigated in Zabala, *The Remains of Being*.

74. Gianni Vattimo, *La vita dell'altro: Bioetica senza metafisica* (Lungro di Cosenza: Marco Editore, 2006). See also the essay of M. G. Weiss, "What's Wrong with Biotechnology? Vattimo's Interpretation of Science, Technology and the Media," in Benso and Schroeder, *Between Nihilism and Politics*.

75. Hilary Putnam, *Ethics Without Ontology* (Cambridge Mass.: Harvard University Press 2004).

76. I have tried to develop the question of the public role of nihilism along these lines in Franca D'Agostini, *The Last Fumes: Nihilism and the Nature of Philosophical Concepts* (Aurora, CO: Davies Group Publications, 2009).

77. Gianni Vattimo, *Addio alla verità* (Rome: Meltemi, 2009).

78. See Franca D'Agostini, "Vattimo's Theory of Truth," in Benso and Schroeder, *Between Nihilism and Politics*.

79. Gianni Vattimo, *Ecce comu* (Rome: Fazi, 2007).

80. See specifically Arendt's *Responsibility and Judgement*, ed. J. Kohn (New York: Schocken, 2003).

81. I wish to thank William McCuaig for giving me the opportunity to review and substantially revise his draft translation of the introduction I wrote in Italian in 2000; and for reviewing my English draft of this postscript.

1. [The contrast adduced in the original Italian is between *una scienza* and *un sapere*. The word *scienza* has the same range of generic and specific meanings as "science" in English: it literally and generically means "a knowing," and by extension and specifically, one of the knowledge disciplines. *Un sapere* means the same thing as *un savoir* in French, and I usually employ an expansion such as "form of knowledge" or "way of knowing" to translate it. *Un sapere* in turn contrasts with *una conoscenza (une connaissance)*, which means "acquaintance, familiarity, knowledge as cognizance," but the contrast is harder to maintain in English, where normal usage requires that *conoscenza/connaissance* be translated simply as "knowledge." WM]

2. Martin Heidegger, "The Age of the World Picture," in *Off the Beaten Track*, ed. and trans. Julian Young and Kenneth Haynes (New York: Cambridge University Press, 2002), 57–73 and appendices, 73–85. ["Die Zeit des Weltbildes" (1938), in *Holzwege*, ed. Friedrich-Wilhelm von Herrmann (Frankfurt: Vittorio Klostermann, 1977; revised edition 2003; vol. 5 of the Heidegger Gesamtausgabe vol. 5), 75–96, and 96–113.]

3. Hans-Georg Gadamer, *Reason in the Age of Science*, trans. Frederick G. Lawrence (Cambridge, Mass: MIT Press, 1981). [*Vernunft im Zeitalter der Wissenschaft: Aufsätze* (Frankfurt: Suhrkamp, 1976).]

4. Gadamer, "What is Practice? The Conditions of Social Reason," in *Reason in the Age of Science*, 85. ["Was ist Praxis? Die Bedingungen gesellschaftlicher Vernunft," in *Vernunft im Zeitalter der Wissenschaft*, 74–75.]

5. In *The Adventure of Difference* I had this to say about the meaning of *Ge-Stell* in Heidegger: "In German the word *Gestell* ordinarily has the meaning of 'pedestal, shelves, framework,' but Heidegger treats it as though it were a compound of *Ge* and *Stell.* . . . *Ge-Stell* is the ensemble of the [meanings of the verb] *stellen*, 'to set in place.' The technological world is the world in which Being is posed/disposed/imposed/composed." The *Adventure of Difference*, 169. [I have modified the Blamires translation considerably. WM]

6. Martin Heidegger, "Der Satz der Identität," 27, in *Identität und Differenz* (Neske: Pfullingen, 1957), 9–30, here at 27. (*Identität und Differenz* is also published in vol. 11 of the Heidegger Gesamtausgabe, 2006). "Der Satz der Identität" consists of the "unchanged text" of a lecture delivered by Heidegger at the University of Freiburg-im-Breisgau on June 27, 1957.

7. Martin Heidegger, "The Principle of Identity," in *Identity and Difference*, trans. and intro. by Joan Stambaugh (New York: Harper and Row, 1969), 23–41, here at 38. Note Stambaugh's translation of *Ge-Stell* as "frame."

8. See Heidegger, "The Age of the World Picture," in *Off the Beaten Track*, 72–73. ["Die Zeit des Weltbildes" (1938), in *Holzwege*, 95–96.]

9. Hans-Georg Gadamer, "I fondamenti filosofici del XX secolo," in *Filosofia '86*, ed. Gianni Vattimo (Rome: Laterza, 1985); original German text: "Die philosophischen Grundlagen des zwanzigsten Jahrhunderts" (1965) in Gadamer, *Neuere philosophie II* (Mohr: Tübingen, 1987; vol. 4 of *Gesammelte Werke*), 3–22.

10. Gianni Vattimo, "Histoire d'une virgule.: Gadamer et le sens de l'être," in *Revue internationale de philosophie* 54 (2000): 499–513.

The Italian text: "Storia di una virgola. Gadamer e il senso dell'essere," in *Iride* 2000, no. 2: 323–336.

11. Hans-Georg Gadamer, *Wahrheit und Methode: Grundzuge einer philosophischen Hermeneutik* (Tubingen: J. C. B. Mohr, 1972), 450 (italics in the original).

12. In fact the published Italian and English translations both leave them out: "L'essere che può venir compreso è linguaggio." Hans-Georg Gadamer, *Verità e metodo*, trans. Gianni Vattimo (Milan: Bompiani, 1983), 542. "Being that can be understood is language." Hans-Georg Gadamer, *Truth and Method*, 2nd rev. edition, trans. revised by Joel Weinsheimer and Donald G. Marshall (New York: Continuum, 2004), 470.

13. Heidegger, *Sein und Zeit*, ed. Friedrich-Wilhelm von Herrmann (Frankfurt: Vittorio Klostermann, 1977; vol. 2 of the Heidegger Gesamtausgabe vol. 2), 304.

14. Heidegger, *Being and Time*, trans. Joan Stambaugh (Albany: SUNY Press, 1996), 211. [I follow the common practice in English of capitalizing the noun "Being" when it translates *Sein* and using the lower-case "being" when it translates *das Seiende*. Joan Stambaugh, the distinguished translator of Heidegger, rejects this practice for reasons she explains in her foreword, but for the sake of consistency I have modified her translation here, capitalizing "Being." In Italian, or Vattimo's Italian anyway, *Sein* is translated by *essere*, and *das Seiende* by *esseri* ("beings") or *ente* (*ens*, thing in existence), while *Dasein* is translated by *l'Esserci*. In the case at hand, Vattimo adapts "Sein–nicht Seiendes" into the form "essere-non-ente." WM]

15. Gianfrancesco Zanetti, *Felicità amicizia diritto* (Rome: Carocci, 1998).

16. An English translation of Edmund Husserl's *Philosophie als strenge Wissenschaft* is available in Husserl, *Philosophy as Rigorous Science,* in *Phenomenology and the Crisis of Philosophy: Philosophy as Rigorous Science and Philosophy and the Crisis of European Man*, trans. Quentin Lauer (New York: Harper and Row, 1965), 71–147.

2. PHILOSOPHY, HISTORY, LITERATURE

1. "Truth and Rhetoric in Hermeneutic Ontology" (1984), in *The End of Modernity*, chap. 8. See also chap. 1, "An Apology for Nihilism."

2. Nietzsche, *Beyond Good and Evil*, aphorism 22.

3. ["Sciences of the spirit" translates as *Geisteswissenschaften*. WM]

3. LOGIC IN PHILOSOPHY

1. An Italian-born mathematician and student of phenomenology, he taught at MIT for many years and died in 1998; see Giancarlo Rota, *Indiscrete Thoughts*, ed. Fabrizio Palombi (Boston: Birkhauser, 1997).

2. See Carlo Ossola, *Le antiche memorie del nulla* (Rome: Edizioni di storia e letteratura, 1997); and Nathan J. Jun, "The letter of Fredegisus of Tours on Nothingness and Shadow: A New Translation and Commentary," *Comitatus* 34 (2003): 150–69.

4. TO SPEAK THE TRUTH

1. "You have redeemed us, Lord God of truth." Psalm 31:5–6. In the Latin Bible, or Vulgate, from which Vattimo quotes, this is Psalm 30.

2. Richard Rorty, *Truth and Progress* (Cambridge: Cambridge University Press, 1998). [Mention may also be made of Richard Rorty and Pascal Engel, *What's the Use of Truth?*, ed. Patrick Savidan, trans. William McCuaig (New York: Columbia University Press, 2007). WM]

5. THE VOCATION TO PHILOSOPHY AND THE RESPONSIBILITY OF PHILOSOPHY

1. [See Gianni Vattimo with Piergiorgio Paterlini, *Not Being God: A Collaborative Autobiography*, trans. William McCuaig (New York: Columbia University Press, 2009) for an account of the philosopher's youth. WM]

2. *Credere di credere* (Milan: Garzanti, 1996); *Belief*, trans. Luca D'Isanto and David Webb (Stanford: Stanford University Press, 2000).

3. Jacques Derrida, "Faith and Knowledge: The Two Sources of 'Religion' at the Limits of Reason Alone," trans. Samuel Weber, in Jacques Derrida and Gianni Vattimo, ed., *Religion* (Stanford: Stanford University Press, 1998), 1–78, here at 4.

4. See Richard Rorty, *Contingency, Irony, Solidarity* (New York: Cambridge University Press, 1989). See esp. chap. 6, "From ironist theory to private allusions: Derrida," 122–137.

5. Rorty, *Contingency, Irony, Solidarity*, 125.

6. Published as *Il concetto di fare in Aristotele* (Turin: Giapicchelli, 1961); in Vattimo, *Ermeneutica*. Vol. 1, *Opere Complete*. Edited by Mario Cedrini, A. Martinengo, and Santiago Zabala. Meltemi: Rome, 2007, 19–180.

7. Luigi Pareyson, *Estetica: Teoria della formatività*, 2nd ed. (Milan: Bompiani, 1988; 1st ed. 1954).

8. "Man kann den Philosophen vielleicht als denjenigen bezeichnen, der das aufnehmende und reagierende Organ für die Ganzheit des Seins hat. . . . einen Sinn für die Gesamtheit der Dinge und des Lebens." Georg Simmel, *Hauptprobleme der Philosophie* (New York: Albert Unger, 1920), 12.

BIBLIOGRAPHY

The entries for the works of certain authors, including Gadamer, Heidegger, and Vattimo himself, are headed by the title of the English translation where that has been cited in the text. Bibliographical information about the corresponding editions in the original language, which are also cited in the text in some cases, or translations in other languages, is supplied immediately after in square brackets.

Antiseri, Dario. *Le ragioni del pensiero debole. Domande a Gianni Vattimo*. Rome: Borla, 1993.

Arendt, Hannah. *Responsibility and Judgement*. Edited by Jerome Kohn. New York: Schocken, 2003.

Basti, Gianfranco, and Antonio Perrone. *Le radici forti del pensiero debole: Nichilismo e fondamenti della matematica*. Con-tratto, 1992.

Benso, Silvia, and Brian Schroeder, eds. *Between Nihilism and Politics: The Hermeneutics of Gianni Vattimo*. Albany: SUNY Press 2009.

Berti, Enrico. *Le vie della ragione*. Bologna: Il Mulino, 1987.

Borruti, Francesco. "Pensiero della differenza: Il nichilismo di Gilles Deleuze." In Melchiorre, *La differenza e l'origine*.

Brandom, Robert. *Making It Explicit: Reasoning, Representing, and Discursive Commitment.* Cambridge, MA: Harvard University Press, 1997.

Ciancio, Claudio. *Il paradosso della verità.* Turin: Rosenberg and Sellier, 1999.

D'Agostini, Franca. *Analitici e continentali.* Milan: Raffaello Cortina, 1997.

——. *The Last Fumes: Nihilism and the Nature of Philosophical Concepts.* Aurora, CO: Davies Group Publications, 2009.

——. "Theoria, teoria, transtheoria." *Lettera Matematica Pristem* 30 (1999).

——. "Vattimo's Theory of Truth." In Benso and Schroeder, *Between Nihilism and Politics.*

Deleuze, Gilles. *Critique et clinique.* Paris: Éditions de Minuit, 1993.

——. *Difference and Repetition.* Translated by Paul Patton. New York: Columbia University Press, 1994. [*Différence et répétition.* Paris: PUF, 2008. First published 1968.]

——. *Nietzsche and Philosophy.* Rev. ed. Translated by Hugh Tomlinson. New York: Columbia University Press, 2006. [*Nietzsche et la philosophie.* Paris: PUF, 2005. First published 1962.]

Derrida, Jacques. "Faith and Knowledge: The Two Sources of 'Religion' at the Limits of Reason Alone." *Religion.* Edited by Jacques Derrida and Gianni Vattimo, translated by Samuel Weber, , 1–78. Stanford: Stanford University Press, 1998.

——. *Writing and Difference.* Translated by Alan Bass. London: Routledge and Kegan Paul, 1978. [*L'écriture et la différence.* Paris: Seuil, 1967. *La scrittura e la differenza.* Translated by Gianni Pozzi, introduction by Gianni Vattimo. Turin: Einaudi, 1998.]

Engel, Pascal. "The Decline and Fall of French Nietzscheo-Structuralism." In *European Philosophy and the American Academy,* edited by

Barry Smith. LaSalle, IL: The Hegeler Institute/The Monist
Library of Philosophy, 1994.

Ferraris, M. *Differenze. La filosofia francese dopo lo strutturalismo*. Milan: Multhipla, 1981.

Fish, Stanley. *The Trouble with Principle*. Cambridge, MA: Harvard University Press, 1999.

Fornero, Giovanni. "Postmoderno e filosofia." In *Storia della Filosofia*, edited by Nicola Abbagnano, vol. 4.2. Turin: UTET, 1996.

Gadamer, Hans Georg. "Die philosophischen Grundlagen des zwanzigsten Jahrhunderts." In Gadamer, *Gesammelte Werke* vol. 4; *Neuere philosophie* vol. 2. Tubingen: J. C. B. Mohr, 1987. ["I fondamenti filosofici del XX secolo." In *Filosofia '86*. Edited by Gianni Vattimo. Rome: Laterza, 1985.]

——. *Reason in the Age of Science*. Translated by Frederick G. Lawrence. Cambridge, MA: MIT Press, 1981. [*Vernunft im Zeitalter der Wissenschaft: Aufsätze*. Frankfurt: Suhrkamp, 1976.] See esp. "What is Practice? The Conditions of Social Reason" ["Was ist Praxis? Die Bedingungen gesellschaftlicher Vernunft."].

——. *Truth and Method*. 2nd rev. ed. Translation revised by Joel Weinsheimer and Donald G. Marshall. New York: Continuum, 2004. [*Wahrheit und Methode*: *Grundzuge einer philosophischen Hermeneutik*. Tubingen: J. C. B. Mohr, 1972. *Verità e metodo*. Translated by Gianni Vattimo. Milan: Bompiani, 1983.]

Giorgio, Giovanni. *Il pensiero di Gianni Vattimo: L'emancipazione dalla metafisica tra dialettica ed ermeneutica*. Milan: Franco Angeli, 2006.

Guarino, Thomas G. *Vattimo and Theology*. New York: T & T Clark, 2009.

Heidegger, Martin. *Being and Time*. Translated by Joan Stambaugh. Albany: SUNY Press, 1996. [*Sein und Zeit*. Edited by

Friedrich-Wilhelm von Herrmann. Frankfurt: Vittorio Klostermann, 1977. Heidegger Gesamtausgabe vol. 2.]

——. *Identity and Difference*. Translated with an introduction by Joan
Stambaugh. New York: Harper and Row, 1969. [*Identität und
Differenz*. Neske: Pfullingen, 1957. Also in vol. 11 of the Heidegger
Gesamtausgabe.] See esp. "The Principle of Identity" ["Der Satz
der Identität"].

——. *Martin Heidegger Gesamtausgabe*. 102 vols. Frankfurt: Vittorio Klostermann, 1975-. See: http://www.klostermann.de/heidegger/
gesamt.htm.

——. *Off the Beaten Track*. Edited and Translated by Julian Young and
Kenneth Haynes. New York: Cambridge University Press, 2002.
[*Holzwege*. Edited by Friedrich-Wilhelm von Herrmann. Frank-
furt: Vittorio Klostermann, 1977; rev. ed. 2003. Heidegger Gesam-
tausgabe vol. 5 .] See esp. "The Age of the World Picture" ["Die
Zeit des Weltbildes"].

——. *Pathmarks*. Edited and translated by William McNeil. New York:
Cambridge University Press, 1998. [*Wegmarken*. Edited by
Friedrich-Wilhelm von Herrmann; Frankfurt: Vittorio Klos-
termann, 1976; rev. ed. 1996. Heidegger Gesamtausgabe vol. 9].
See esp. "On the Essence of Ground" ["Vom Wesen des
Grundes"].

Husserl, Edmund. *Phenomenology and the Crisis of Philosophy: Philosophy as Rigorous Science and Philosophy and the Crisis of European Man*. Translated by Quentin Lauer. New York: Harper and
Row, 1965.

Jun, Nathan J. "The Letter of Fredegisus of Tours on Nothingness and
Shadow: A New Translation and Commentary." *Comitatus* 34
(2003): 150–69.

Kosok, Michel. "La formalizzazione della logica dialettica hegeliana." In *La formalizzazione della dialettica. Hegel, Marx, e la logica contemporanea*, edited by Diego Marconi. Turin: Rosenberg and Sellier, 1979.

Lyotard, Jean-François. *Des dispositifs pulsionnels*. Paris: Bourgois, 1980.

——. *The Postmodern Condition: A Report on Knowledge*. Translated by Geoff Bennington and Brian Massumi, foreword by Fredric Jameson. Minneapolis: University of Minnesota Press, 1984. [*La condition postmoderne: Rapport sur le savoir*. Paris: Éditions de Minuit, 1979.]

Magris, Aldo. "I forti impegni del pensiero debole. Un seminario di Gianni Vattimo a Venezia." *aut-aut* 273–274 (1996).

Malpas, Jeff, and Santiago Zabala, eds. *Consequences of Hermeneutics: Fifty Years after Truth and Method*. Evanston: Northwestern University Press, 2010.

Melchiorre, Virgilio, ed. *La differenza e l'origine*. Milan: Vita e Pensiero, 1987.

Nietzsche, Friedrich. *The Will to Power*. Translated by R. J. Hollingdale and Walter Kaufmann Edited by Walter Kaufmann. New York: Vintage Books, 1968.

Ossola, Carlo. *Le antiche memorie del nulla*. Rome: Edizioni di storia e letteratura, 1997.

Pareyson, Luigi. "La filosofia e il problema del male." *Annuario filosofico* 2 (1996).

——. *Estetica: Teoria della formatività*. 2nd ed. Milan: Bompiani, 1988; 1st ed., 1954.

Parr, Adrian, ed.. *The Deleuze Dictionary*. New York: Columbia University Press, 2006.

Putnam, Hilary. *Ethics Without Ontology*. Cambridge Mass.: Harvard University Press 2004.

Rorty, Richard. *Contingency, Irony, and Solidarity*. New York: Cambridge University Press, 1989. See esp. chap. 6, "From Ironist Theory to Private Allusions: Derrida."

——. *Truth and Progress*. Cambridge: Cambridge University Press, 1998.

Rota, Giancarlo. *Indiscrete Thoughts*. Edited by Fabrizio Palombi. Boston: Birkhauser, 1997.

Rovatti, Pier Aldo, and Alessandro Dal Lago. *Elogio del pudore: Per un pensiero debole*. Milan: Feltrinelli, 1989.

Severino, Emanuele. *Essenza del nichilismo*. New expanded ed. Milan: Adelphi, 1995; 1st ed., 1972.

——. *Gli abitatori del tempo: Cristianesimo, marxismo, tecnica*. 3rd ed. Rome: Armando, 1989; 1st ed., 1978.

——. *La struttura originaria*. New expanded ed. Milan: Adelphi, 2007; 1st ed., 1958.

Simmel, Georg. *Hauptprobleme der Philosophie*. New York: Albert Unger, 1920.

Sini, Carlo. "Identità e differenza nella filosofia francese contemporanea." In Melchiorre, *La differenza e l'origine*.

Staquet, Anne. *La pensée faible de Vattimo e Rovatti: Une pensée fable*. Paris: L'Harmattan, 1996.

Vattimo, Gianni. *Addio alla verità*. Rome: Meltemi, 2009.

——. The *Adventure of Difference: Philosophy after Nietzsche and Heidegger*. Translated by Cyprian Blamires with the assistance of Thomas Harrison. Baltimore: Johns Hopkins University Press, 1993. [*Le avventure della differenza: Che cosa significa pensare dopo Nietzsche e Heidegger*. Milan: Garzanti, 1980.] See esp. "Dialectic and Difference," "Nietzsche and difference."

——. *Al di là del soggetto: Nietzsche, Heidegger, e la ermeneutica*. Milan: Feltrinelli, 1981.

——. *Belief*. Translated by Luca D'Isanto and David Webb. Stanford: Stanford University Press, 2000. [*Credere di credere*. Milan: Garzanti, 1996.]

——. *Beyond Interpretation: The Meaning of Hermeneutics for Philosophy*. Translated by David Webb. Stanford: Stanford University Press, 1997. [*Oltre l'interpretazione: Il significato della ermeneutica per la filosofia*. Rome: Laterza, 1994.] See esp. "The Nihilistic Vocation of Hermeneutics."

——. *Il concetto di fare in Aristotele*. Turin: Giapicchelli, 1961. Also in Vattimo, *Ermeneutica*. Vol. 1, *Opere Complete*. Edited by Mario Cedrini, Alberto Martinengo, and Santiago Zabala. Meltemi: Rome, 2007, 19–180.

——. "Le deboli certezze." In *Alfabeta* 67 (1984).

——. "Dialettica, differenza, pensiero debole." In Vattimo and Rovatti, *Il Pensiero Debole*.

——. *Dialogue with Nietzsche*. Translated by William McCuaig. New York: Columbia University Press, 2006. [*Dialogo con Nietzsche: Saggi 1961–2000*. Milan: Garzanti, 2000.]

——. "Diritto all'argomentazione." In *Filosofia '92*. Edited by Gianni Vattimo. Rome: Laterza, 1993.

——. *Ecce comu*. Rome: Fazi, 2007.

——. *The End of Modernity: Nihilism and Hermeneutics in Postmodern Culture*. Translated with an introduction by Jon R. Snyder. Baltimore: Johns Hopkins University Press, 1988. [*La fine della modernità: Nichilismo ed ermeneutica nella cultura post-moderna*. Milan: Garzanti, 1985.] See esp. "Nihilism and the Postmodern in Philosophy""An Apology for Nihilism," "Truth and Rhetoric in Hermeneutic Ontology."

——. "Histoire d'une virgule: Gadamer et le sens de l'être." In *Revue internationale de philosophie* 54 (2000), pp. 499–513. ["Storia di una virgola: Gadamer e il senso dell'essere." In *Iride* 2000, no. 2, pp. 323–336.]

——. "L'ontologia ermeneutica nella filosofia contemporanea," Introduction to *Verità e metodo*, by Hans-Georg Gadamer, Translated by Gianni Vattimo. Milan: Bompiani, 1983.

——. "Perché 'debole'." In *Dove va la filosofia italiana?* edited by J. Jacobelli. Rome: Laterza, 1996.

——. "Postilla 1983." Afterword to *Verità e metodo*, by Hans-Georg Gadamer, Translated by Gianni Vattimo. Milan: Bompiani, 1983.

——. *La vita dell'altro: Bioetica senza metafisica*. Lungro di Cosenza: Marco Editore, 2006.

Vattimo, Gianni, and Pier Aldo Rovatti, eds. *Il Pensiero Debole*. Milan: Feltrinelli, 1983.

Vattimo, Gianni and Richard Rorty. *The Future of Religion*. Edited by Santiago Zabala. New York: Columbia University Press, 2005.

Vattimo, Gianni and Piergiorgio Paterlini. *Not Being God: A Collaborative Autobiography*. Translated by William McCuaig. New York: Columbia University Press, 2009. [*Non essere Dio: Un' autobiografia a quattro mani*. Reggio Emilia: Aliberti, 2006.]

Wang, H. *A Logical Journey. From Gödel to Philosophy*. Cambridge, Mass.: MIT Press, 1996.

Weiss, M. G. "What's Wrong with Biotechnology? Vattimo's Interpretation of Science, Technology and the Media." In *Between Nihilism and Politics*, Benso and Schroeder eds.

Yourgrau, P. *The Disappearance of Time. Kurt Gödel and the Idealistic Tradition of Philosophy*. New York: Cambridge University Press, 1991.

Zabala, Santiago. *The Remains of Being: Hermeneutic Ontology after Metaphysics*. New York: Columbia University Press, 2009.

Zabala, Santiago, ed. *Weakening Philosophy: Essays in Honour of Gianni Vattimo*. Montreal: McGill-Queen's University Press, 2007.

Zanetti, Gianfrancesco. *Felicità amicizia diritto*. Rome: Carocci, 1998.

143

BIBLIOGRAPHY

INDEX